HEAD CASE

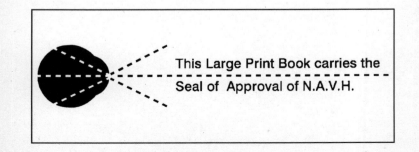

This Large Print Book carries the Seal of Approval of N.A.V.H.

HEAD CASE

MY BRAIN AND OTHER WONDERS

COLE COHEN

THORNDIKE PRESS

A part of Gale, Cengage Learning

Farmington Hills, Mich • San Francisco • New York • Waterville, Maine
Meriden, Conn • Mason, Ohio • Chicago

GALE
CENGAGE Learning®

LIBRARY OF CONGRESS CATALOGING-IN-PUBLICATION DATA

Cohen, Cole.
     Head case : my brain and other wonders / by Cole Cohen. — Large Print
edition.
      pages cm
    ISBN 978-1-4104-8086-6 (hardcover) — ISBN 1-4104-8086-0 (hardcover)
     1. Cohen, Cole. 2. Brain—Abnormalities—Patients—United States—
Biography. 3. Young women—United States—Biography. 4. Women with
disabilities—United States—Biography. 5. Learning disabled—United
States—Biography. 6. Large type books. I. Title.
RC395.C57 2015b
616.80092—dc23
[B]   2015013731

Published in 2015 by arrangement with Henry Holt and Company, LLC

For anyone who has ever felt invisible

A labyrinth is an ancient device that compresses a journey into a small space, winds a path like a thread on a spool. It contains beginning, confusion, perseverance, arrival, and return. There at last the metaphysical journey of your life and your actual movements are one and the same. You may wander, you may learn that in order to get to your destination you must turn away from it, become lost, spin about, and then only after the way has become overwhelming and absorbing, arrive, having gone the great journey without having gone far from the ground.

— Rebecca Solnit, *The Faraway Nearby*

■ ■ ■ ■

I.
BEGINNING

■ ■ ■ ■

"It'll be no use putting their heads down and saying, 'Come up again, dear!' I shall only look up and say 'Who am I, then? Tell me that first and then, if I like being that person, I shall come up; if not, I'll stay down here until I'm somebody else' — but, oh dear!" cried Alice, with a sudden burst of tears, "I do wish they would put their heads down! I am so very tired of being all alone here!"

— Lewis Carroll, *Alice in Wonderland*

NEUROLOGY EXAM

May 2, 2007
Portland, Oregon

Inside my stomach it feels bright and cold like those old cartoons where the crow swallows a mercury thermometer and reels around the room clutching his gut, hiccupping in percussive squeals. My purse is clamped tightly under my arm; the gold clasp digs into my armpit. I am with my father — or my mother; I don't remember who drove me and who was at work. I didn't drive myself because I can't; which is why I'm here. I'm not moving to Southern California for grad school without knowing first how to drive, and since I was fifteen no one's been able to teach me how to and no one, including me, has been able to reason out what's stopping me. When I try to drive I get disoriented, overwhelmed, and tired, but doesn't everyone at first? Both parents will be summoned to the next appointment.

I think that my mother was with me. She's the one who teased out the first thread by calling the Physical Therapy Department of Providence Hospital; where we are now, but instead we're in the Neurology Department. When my mother called Physical Therapy asking to speak to an occupational therapist about my symptoms (disorientation, exhaustion, not knowing left from right, not understanding where to place my hands on the steering wheel during a three-point turn) and to schedule an appointment with a driving specialist, the occupational therapist who answered the phone told her that my symptoms sounded neurological. In retrospect this sounds obvious, but of course, in retrospect it all sounds so obvious. In this waiting room, where I am the youngest person by forty years other than my mother because the neurologist specializes in "geriatric assessment," nobody knows anything yet. We're all sitting together in the cell reserved for anticipation.

The physical therapist recommended that I see Dr. Volt, who is known for "solving puzzles." The scheduling happens around me during phone calls that are later reiterated to me. I fill out paperwork, sign medical information release forms, mail them to the receptionist, and wait.

This afternoon we wait for half an hour I think, but since I'm particularly inept at calculating time as it passes I can't be sure of this either. The wait feels simultaneously slow and fast; interminable and bound to be over far too soon. I don't especially look forward to being granted entrance to the other side of that door.

This is an experiment for all involved: the neurologist, my parents, me. The previous evidence, stacked in a filing cabinet in my parents' garage, suggests that this is another pointless exercise. The first file (*Testing — Dyslexia*) dates back to kindergarten. There's also middle school (*Testing — ADD/ADHD*) and high school (*Testing — Motor Visual, Testing — Vision*). The files are full of my handwriting samples in both print and cursive, my drawings of squares overlapping circles, Scantron sheets, more drawings that I made when a school psychologist asked me to show her what a "happy girl" looks like, what my family looks like; the "happy girl" has wings and wears a crown. There are yellowing copies of worksheets with the prompts "I am good at:" and "I am bad at:", unsolved math problems, and pages of typed notes from various school district learning specialists. In the file dedicated to my driving issues, there are old failed tests, flashcards, and handbooks. My parents are both researchers. My mother is a librarian and my dad is a philosophy professor; I am their longest-running joint research project.

I imagine a long-running quiz show, led by a host with a fiberglass smile and a skinny mic. *Name That Learning Disability* has been on-air since 1984, when it took me several months to learn how to tie my shoes in kindergarten. It's been running since then, featuring episodic intervals of test bubbles to fill in, blocks to stack in the correct pattern, flashcards to name.

Each round of testing was gingerly posited to me with the same phrasing. "We're just trying to figure out what's really going on." What's really going on is that I am horrible at math; I don't know my left from my right; I can't judge distance, time, or space, read maps, travel independently without getting lost; or drive. As long as I've had these issues, I've had coping strategies. You may think that I'm kind of odd in that wacky-professor sort of way. I'd forget my head if it wasn't screwed on straight, et cetera. But you would never realize that as I'm walking next to you down the street, you are leading us both.

The trouble is routine, schedule, structure.

This is why the academic world works well for me, part of why I'm headed to grad school in a couple of months. Semesters, breaks, three-hour classes — it's like having someone cut up my year into small little sections with a knife and fork and feed them to me.

The trouble usually starts with getting anywhere on time. From elementary through high school, getting me out the door and off to school was next to impossible for my mother, a daily ritual of exasperation. Finding all of my books, my other shoe, all a mess.

Once when I was in elementary school, I waited two hours for a school bus that never arrived. I didn't know that it was a snow day, and neither did my mom, who had assumed that I'd gotten on the bus. I don't know when a child gains a sense of time, or if this is something that another child would do. I don't doubt that without a watch I'd do the same thing again, today.

One of the great tensions in my life is in the concept of a reasonable amount of time. Wearing a watch should solve this problem, but how long until I should check my watch again? Is it time yet to check my watch again? Should I wait longer? What about now? No, not yet. Because I swear, if I look

15

at it one more time and it still says that it's been only two minutes since I last checked it, I will scream. Right here, right now, I will crumple up and die. The bus will never come, but I can't leave because I have to get to work; still, I swear I am certain that the bus will never ever arrive. It has been two minutes. It has been an ice age. Dinosaurs have been wiped off the planet, human beings drag their knuckles and scrawl in caves, make fire and learn to walk upright, invent the wheel, create and drive cars, go grocery shopping, and still I'm here waiting for the bus. Check the watch: five minutes. Progress. My life is spent either waiting or leaving someone waiting.

Being on time is a very calculated act for me. I have to focus all of my energy on following sequential actions, "I have to shower, then get dressed, then pack my bag . . . ," and be careful not to get drawn away from the task at hand, or I will lose my connection to time the way a child loses a balloon into the air. I tie time to my wrist; I work hard to stay connected to a world that runs by a clock.

Grocery store shopping or visiting any big block store with never-ending aisles, say Costco, is inviting misadventure. If it weren't for the invention of the cell phone I would be writing this from on top of a ten-year supply of paper towels. I've never been able to keep mental maps of locations, and written maps only confuse me. In stores, especially, I have learned to try to give in to it, to say to myself, "OK, I am about to get hopelessly lost." I am then free to wander about the aisles of DVDs or vacuums like a toddler. The cell phone is an electronic breadcrumb trail allowing me to wander the endless aisles of a Costco or Target freely, one call away from rescue. It's also much more private than the storewide intercom, the terror of my childhood. Getting lost in the store is not nearly as cute to clerks when you are twenty-six. Now I use my cell phone to call to report my location to my party, and then I stick to my mark until rescued.

The trouble is in touch. I can remember the first time being touched or touching any of my friends. The first time I hugged my college roommate, Miranda, was freshman year of college. We were both heading home for our first winter break. She said, "All right, bitch," and put her arms loosely around me. It took me a minute to reciprocate. The first time I touched my friend Nathan, some drunken guy at a party kept jokingly trying to twist his nipple, and Nathan kept brushing him off. They were both trying to keep things in good humor, but it was starting to get tense. He and I were in conversation when the nipple twister attempted to strike again. "Cole! Help!" I put my hands lightly on Nathan's chest so that my hands were drunkenly plucked instead of his nipples.

Touch is a very conscious act for me; it means I like you enough to risk negotiating the space between our bodies. My body in space is hassle enough. There's the issue of pressure, of playfully punching a little too hard. Then there's the issue of time; I'd much rather hug someone for too short a time than too long. Touch opens up a mortifying realm of misunderstandings for someone with an out-of-whack internal compass. So let's just avoid it altogether, or let's have a drink or two or three. Touch becomes less fraught when there's an excuse for my fumbling. When I hug my close friends good-bye, they would be shocked to know that it's premeditated.

The trouble is in wanting: to be touched, to go out alone, to speak plainly of my experience without feeling as if I'm making myself out to be that pale invalid boy from *The Secret Garden* who sat in his wicker wheelchair beneath a tree and couldn't play with the other children. The trouble is in wanting desperately to be believed or understood — that this really is my world — and in simultaneously not wanting to be found out.

When I moved to Portland after college, where my parents had moved from Northern California while I was in school, we did "dry runs" of public transportation routes to work or the grocery store together. I always rehearse new public transportation routes with someone who can point out physical landmarks marking where I should get on or off the bus and what benchmark means I'm halfway there. I write notes for myself: "When you see the gas station, pull the cord for your stop."

My first two years in the city I lived on Southeast Belmont Street, where I could walk the same route to Hawthorne Boulevard, a main shopping street with a large grocery store and several coffee shops and restaurants. I walked the same route every day, never taking shortcuts or winding through neighborhoods, until I moved to Northeast Portland and had to learn a new landscape.

There's a unique pleasure in living free from a solid sense of time or space. I've spent my mornings changing my earrings for the third time before I head out the door, blissfully unaware that I'm half an hour late for my shift at work or my class. I have an all-access pass to the place where time stands still. If dillydallying were an extreme sport, I'd have won the gold medal. There's a lovely self-involved gloss to my mornings, sitting on the edge of the bed spacing out and forgetting that I need to keep moving if I'm going to get anywhere on time. There is also the sense of shame.

I never know where my experience ends and the anxiety brought on by my experience begins. When I was in seventh grade, I wrote a report on ostriches. I was charmed by them because they are tall and long-legged and funny looking with big brown eyes, like mine. Fear can stop you from being kind, to both others and yourself. Ostriches will run like hell at the slightest peripheral sign of predators on the horizon; they will kick you in the shins if you get too close.

I rely on my verbal strengths to hide my vulnerabilities. Panic creates borders; it has charted all of my maps. Fear and avoidance grant the facade of some semblance of control, of safety. I am trying to learn not to fear possibility; still I am certain that I cannot survive being known.

Fear is also biological necessity. A friend

once told me about a study he read somewhere in which ostriches, typically high-strung creatures who rely on panic as a driving force to outrun predators, were prescribed anti-anxiety medication. The medication worked; the ostriches were calm and collected and soon they were gobbled up by lions.

"Nicole . . ." I stand abruptly at the sound of my full name. The receptionist leads me down the hall and takes my weight, height, and blood pressure. She opens the door to a beige room with a table and a chair. I sit in the room and try to pay attention to the book that I brought as I wait for Dr. Volt for what feels like quite a long time. He says that we're just going to do some tests, that it's not a big deal and not to feel nervous. He proposes it as if we were about to spend a day at the mall. I nod and shrug and smile and repeat where needed. We are trying to make each other feel comfortable. I want him to see me as a good patient, and he doesn't want any trouble. He tells me that because this is a teaching hospital, a resident is coming, and that I can dismiss the resident for reasons of privacy if I like. His tone makes it clear that if I choose to do so, I must intend to undermine the future of

Western medicine. I say it is fine, which it is.

The resident is late. I can hear him in the hall apologizing to the receptionist. Something about short notice and the MAX, the Portland light-rail system. The receptionist says to him, "We just thought you'd like to see this."

He strides into the exam room straight out of central casting for a hospital soap opera, holding a paper cup of coffee; his blond hair is in a ponytail, his lab coat perfectly starched, and his black dress shoes are shined. He smiles bashfully at me. If he's going to be here, I am mildly insulted that he's late. Am I not enough of a learning opportunity for Dr. Shiny Blond Ponytail? But the resident stays. Worse, I can tell that Dr. Volt likes him. They trade a conspiratorial glance. Volt leaves for a moment; the resident and I make conversation.

"You're leaving for grad school in September?" he asks.

I nod. "CalArts."

"Oh, in Los Angeles."

"In Valencia. Sort of a suburb of LA."

He nods. "Where did you do your undergrad?"

I respond, "Redlands."

"Oh." Silence. "My car broke down in

22

Redlands, once," he offers.

"That sounds about right."

My senior year of college the town got a Chipotle, which was a cause for celebration. There's no way I'm going to live in another dead-end California town without being able to drive myself away from it.

I smile. He smiles. There is a strange current in our conversation because we must be the same age, only he is a doctor and I am a patient. We each have assigned roles here, but on any given Saturday night he could spill his microbrew on me in a crowded bar. Dr. Volt works mostly with Alzheimer's patients; the receptionist has been telling my mother for months on the phone how excited they all are to have a young person come in.

Dr. Volt returns, does his line again about a few tests and not to worry, I do my nod-shrug-smile shuffle, and we begin. He asks me to follow his fingers with my eyes, to name animals, any animals — as many as I can. He mumbles something to the resident. It sounds to me like "Craniolobeneurotemporalocular," to which the resident nods and responds, "neurolobecraniotemporalmatter." Dr. Volt sits very close to me, taps on each of my arms, and asks me to tell him which arm he is tapping on. Then he does the same with each of my fingers on each hand. There is more neurological terminology chatter between them. I am starting to get annoyed. I look Dr. Volt straight in the eye and say, "You're going to explain all of this to me later, right?" He looks at me as if I've spoken out of turn. "We'll talk about this at the end of the exam."

He asks me to place my palm out flat, tells me that he will draw numbers on my palm with his finger.

"What number is this?" he asks.

"Eight."

"And this?"

"One."

"And this?"

"Zero. Zero. And I think that one's zero too."

They start to get excited. The three of us walk to the hallway outside, where Dr. Volt tells me to walk away from them, then toward them. Then on my heels, on my toes. I overhear Dr. Volt say to the resident "see the duck walk, the stiffening of the gait . . ." I become self-conscious and loosen up at the knees. "There, now it's gone."

Though they're trying to hide it from me, I can tell they're really getting worked up, and I'm getting excited too, though I don't know why we're all so excited. The tension mounts with each test; I feel like the quarterback on our little winning football team about to make the winning neurological touchdown; after I walk up and down the hall again we'll all high-five and throw the contents of the waiting-room water cooler over our heads. Instead, the end of the exam catches me by surprise. The resident leaves, and Dr. Volt takes me back to the room and tells me to talk to the receptionist about when to schedule my neuropsychological testing. I feel a bit let down, even a little used. I want to say, "Guys? Wait? Hey, guys? Do you want to, like, get coffee? Oh right, you already have coffee. I see."

I try to stall Dr. Volt as he jots some final notes on my chart. "I'm used to leaving a doctor's office with . . . something. A diagnosis. Could you at least tell me what you saw? Did you . . . gather any important information?" He looks up from his notes and laughs. "Well, we won't really know anything until we get back your MRI and neuropsych testing. And maybe a PET scan . . . Then we'll all meet to discuss the results." I stare at him blankly. "Here, go home and Google this." He writes something on his prescription pad, tears off the page, and hands it to me.

"But I am often wrong," he adds. "Don't hold me to it."

On the slip of paper he's written "Gerstmann's Syndrome." I think, *Oh good, I have a syndrome.* A syndrome feels as if it grants me more purchase than a learning disability, although really it's just a new name for the same set of symptoms.

I may have a rare neurological disorder, a mysterious condition, the main signifier of which is the inability to tell my pointer from my pinky.

What Is Gerstmann's Syndrome?
Gerstmann's syndrome is a neurological disorder . . . characterized by four primary symptoms: a writing disability (agraphia or dysgraphia), a lack of understanding of the rules for calculation or arithmetic (acalculia or dyscalculia), an inability to distinguish right from left, and an inability to identify fingers (finger agnosia).

This is the first description that I find when I punch "Developmental Gerstmann's Syndrome" into Google's search field, translated from Dr. Volt's scrawl. The definition is from the Web site for the National

Institute of Neurological Disorders and Stroke.

Gerstmann's has the feel of a hot-dog diagnosis, stitched from a pile of leftovers. Take a tube filled with bovine guts; where some see a hot dog, others see a cow. Both would be right. Some doctors believe in syndrome as an end-point diagnosis, and others see it merely as a diagnostic tool to get to the heart of a larger illness.

Digging further, I find a June 1966 paper published in a medical journal called simply *Brain*. The medical investigation, "The Enigma of Gerstmann's Syndrome," begins with a quote from the French author André Maurois: "The members of the medical fraternity can at least classify our ailments in carefully labeled compartments, and that, in itself, is reassuring. To be able to call a demon by its name is half-way to getting rid of him."

This quote seems to be intended as ironic because the author, the neurologist Macdonald Critchley, goes on, as best as I can understand, to tear apart the diagnostic framework created by Josef Gerstmann as a combination of symptoms that may not make up a stand-alone syndrome. To my understanding, it's the difference between a Pu-pu platter, a dish made up of smaller appetizers, and an entrée. I don't know what this means for me, what the difference is between having symptoms or a syndrome at this point really, anyway.

"Nooooo . . . don't get an MRIIIIII!" my younger sister, Carly, wails into the phone. "On TV, whenever someone gets an MRI, they always have a seizure." Carly is twenty-three. She works for a graphic design company making pamphlets for fancy new condominiums and lives in a nice apartment in the Pearl district of Portland with her cat, Margot. At this moment, I would much rather she put Margot on the phone. "Carly, put Margot on the phone." Margot whines and breathes heavily but does not foresee imminent peril.

MRI Scan

May 6, 2007

A few days after my first appointment, my dad drives me to a different wing of the same hospital. It's a Sunday; the imaging wing of the hospital is barren. We have to rely on signs to lead us to the waiting room for my MRI appointment. Further crippling our endeavor, the coffee stand is unmanned. We circle around the wing three times until we are stopped in our laps by a security guard, who points us toward the MRI station. We lose our way a few more times. I debate with my dad the difference between an MRI and an X-ray. My win saves us from sitting in the wrong waiting room. I imagine that if my dad were here alone on a Sunday, he would have sat in that waiting room for hours, riffling through moldy copies of *Good Housekeeping* and becoming increasingly irate before walking out in a fury. The similarities between the two of us are well known in our family. We are generally not allowed to go out on errands together, but my mom is working at the library today.

There is no one at the MRI check-in desk, only a large sign instructing us to PRESS BUTTON AND WAIT. If only they had an equally large sign directing us to this button. We both search on, above, and below the desk. Dad begins to repeatedly press the desk, the phone, the chairs, while loudly making urgent buzzing noises. When all else fails, act out. It's a proven strategy, often provoking an immediate response to be negotiated into aid. I'll stop doing what you don't like if you work toward my goals.

Surprisingly, no orderly or security guard comes to quiet his imaginary buzzer. Eventually we find a big red button on the wall, accompanied by the sign PRESS BUTTON HERE.

The hospital is mocking us, I am certain of it. We are being taking advantage of for the pleasures of the Sunday staff. Dr. Volt is looking down upon us from hidden cameras, taking notes and giggling gleefully with his resident, their eyes glazed over with manic joy.

My dad presses the actual button, and an amiable curly-haired twentysomething attendant in dark blue scrubs arrives at the check-in desk. "The button is hard to find," Dad grumbles by way of greeting before slouching into a waiting-room chair. The attendant walks me down the hall to where the MRI machine is housed, making small talk about how our birthdays are close together and cracking unmemorable jokes. He takes me to a small changing station. "You'll need to leave anything with metal in it here." He pushes back the cloth drape and walks away. I part with my hair band, my belt, and, with resignation, my underwire bra.

If you've never had an MRI, here are two contradictory facts to know: it's very loud, and you must lie very still for half an hour. You are given earplugs, which mainly serve as a placebo. The machine never makes this sound on medical dramas because you can't speak over it but in actuality the sound of a processing MRI machine closely resembles industrial music from the mid-1990s: repetitive, patterned, mechanical buzzing at various low frequencies, sometimes broken up by long, grinding atonal drones.

Trent Reznor stars in the music video I make for my MRI while lying very still. He is backlit in a light blue antiseptic shade of neon light, looking sternly into the camera. Reznor's cameo is spliced with black-and-white medical imaging of my brain, which is interrupted by the requisite stuttering jump cut to graphic footage of ongoing brain surgery. When I grow bored with that and start to become really aggravated by the process, I pretend to be in a space shuttle. If you ever have an MRI, at some point during the procedure it is obligatory that you pretend that you are being shot into space. It won't provide a great deal of entertainment, but it will help you keep your sanity while lying very still enclosed in a metal tube forced to listen to grating, repetitive mechanical bursts at great volume.

The curly-haired waiting-room attendant had befriended my dad while I was in the tube, telling him stories of past patients. Dad and I say good-bye to his new friend and head for the car.

"He was funny," I say absently on the way home, looking out the car window.

"I think he liked you."

"I guess that's why he asked me to take off my bra."

PET Scan

The MRI takes pictures of your brain as a static organ — you could take an MRI of a dead person's brain. But a PET scan captures brain activity or inactivity. A PET scan is a test that doctors on TV shows don't order as often as MRIs. The process of performing a PET scan isn't as dramatic or compelling. I have heard the term before, but I don't really know what one is, even as I arrive for my appointment. The technician wears pink scrubs and white sneakers with pink laces and has pink streaks in her hair. I'll call her Pink. She leads me to a small, closetlike room with a cot in it. She has some papers, which she repeatedly ruffles and refers to. I don't care what's on anyone's papers about me anymore.

"Have you had a PET scan before?" asks Pink.

"Um, no."

"OK, well, we're going to put this fluid in your body, and it will tell us if the cancer is still there."

I laugh nervously. "No, you see, there is no . . . I don't have . . ."

She looks at me skeptically. "Well, that's what the doctor put down as a possibility on your chart."

I laugh harder, then harder. I need her to join in to signal that she's in on this joke, but she stares blankly at me. I'm alone in this coat-closet room in a hospital laughing with relief so hard that I'm going to cry because I'm so scared of cancer, scared of death. It's as if this misunderstanding could call the cancer into being and only our shared laughter will keep it at bay. I'm scared of being mistaken for someone who is dying quickly because I'm not ready to think of myself as someone who is dying ever, at all. I take a deep breath and reiterate my stance. "He just put that on there to get the test covered by insurance."

She grudgingly accepts my angle. "So . . . why are you here?"

I stammer through "Motor . . . spatial" — I make a motion with my hands like teasing out a Jenga puzzle piece — "issues."

"Oh." Pink shrugs and begins to set up the bag of radioactive fluid to stick in my arm. I'm startled to see that it's bright blue, and I'm now a little scared.

Pink tells me to lie down, not to move. After she links my arm to this bag of fluid that I really don't want inside me, she turns the lights off and tells me to close my eyes and stay calm. This is my penultimate test; everyone keeps poking me and prodding me and telling me I have cancer or a rare neurological condition but that I must stay still and remain calm.

My youngest sister, Marni, is the only one available to pick me up after my PET scan.

Getting Marni to agree to give me a ride is like physically ripping a train off the tracks with your bare arms. She is eighteen and has better things to do than pick up her twenty-six-year-old sister from the hospital. I'm certain that she'll be late and quietly seething. Things have been tense between us since earlier this summer, when I spotted something anatomically amiss under her shirt and blurted out "Are your *nipples* pierced?" in front of our mom. But here, in this dark closet, I must not think unnerving thoughts. I can feel the cold neon poison traveling through my circuitry. I am tired, weepy, scared, detached, and amused, and I am doing my best to remain calm.

Pink returns to flip on the lights. She

walks me into a large room with a machine shaped like a doughnut and explains that I am to lie still inside it on a plastic plank as they take pictures of my brain. The blue tracer will highlight in the images the parts of my brain that are working.

I already know what it is that I don't know: how long an hour is, how wide a doorway, how to find the peanut butter in the supermarket, how to calculate a tip, how to tie my shoes correctly, how to get back home without getting lost on the way. How do you explain how long an hour is to someone? How do you describe the passage of sixty minutes; two sitcoms or maybe one cable drama? What can you get done in an hour? How long is an hour to wait? Have I been at the hospital for more than an hour this afternoon?

What I do know: an hour is usually too far to drive somewhere last minute. It's not enough time to get much schoolwork done. It's very, very, very late if you were supposed to meet someone the hour beforehand. It's the amount of time I give myself to get ready in the morning. Sometimes it's too much time to get ready; sometimes it's not enough.

Standing outside of the glass doors of the hospital while waiting for Marni to pick me up, I watch a woman wheel her IV drip bag through the small rose garden by the parking lot. She repeatedly navigates her cigarette between a maze of crisscrossing tubes and into her mouth.

Neuropsychiatric Inventory

June 13, 2007

This is the same battery of tests that I've been given since elementary school, copying shapes, defining vocabulary words, some basic math, a few memory games. They're supposed to measure concentration, reasoning, problem solving, and memory. When I was younger, the tests weren't explained much beyond the reassurance that it's all to help make school easier for me, so I shouldn't be nervous about them. The eraser on my pencil always tears through the same rough brown scratch paper that I'm given every time to figure out the arithmetic problems on. I still remember the pride that I felt during my first round of exams in elementary school when the tester held up a picture of an Asian-style building, asking me to name it, and "pagoda" jumped out of my mouth.

It usually takes a couple days to complete

the tests, but today we're going to get them done in one long day. I've never been able to sit through them without feeling as if I'm on trial. No matter how many times I've taken them and how much older I am each time, these tests always terrify me. What are they really looking for? What can they see?

PROVIDENCE COGNITIVE ASSESSMENT CLINIC

Current meds (prescribed by outside physician):

Seroquel 100 mg tabs (Quetiapine Fumarate)
Lamictal 100 mg tabs (Lamotrigine)
Rozerem 8 mg tabs (Ramelteon)
Ativan tabs (Lorazepam)

Neurobehaviorial observations:

Behavior today at clinic: calm, cooperative
Depression: endorses
Anxiety: endorses
Mania: denies
Suicide ideation: denies
Death ideation: denies

If you don't deny, they lock you away for two weeks. Then they let you back out.

DIAGNOSIS

June 17, 2007

I am flanked by my mother and father on the walk out of Dr. Volt's waiting room. He stops us before we get to the exam room, a manila folder under his arm. We're crowded in an awkward cluster in the hall. I have never before felt this precise hybrid of fear and boredom. "Mary," he calls out to the receptionist, "I can't get the MRI to show up on the screen in the exam room. I'll take them to my office instead." I hadn't expected that we would be looking at the MRI images. Because no one called me afterward with the results, I assumed that there were none to speak of. But when you pay for big expensive tests, it does seem like proper medical etiquette to be shown the results.

Dr. Volt takes a few minutes to print out his report and make sure that the computer in his office is running, then he calls us in from the hallway. He is behind his desk; the computer monitor is turned toward us. There are three chairs for us to sit in. I sit in front of the MRI image on the monitor, to the side of the other two chairs. My mom sits next to me, my dad next to her. I don't understand the image in front of me. It's a black-and-white splice of a brain, I assume mine, with an inky black spot on it in the shape of a lopsided heart. I tell myself that this is a spot on the film, which it's way too large to actually be. It's something not to worry about, something I don't understand that the doctor will explain away. The image is too starkly obvious for me to process. The simplicity of it, a big black spot on my brain, renders me speechless.

We are all staring dumbly at the image on the screen until Dr. Volt begins to speak. "So, this is your brain . . . and this" — he points with a pencil to the black spot — "is a hole." The image comes into focus. It is not debatable. There is a large hole in the picture of the brain. The picture of the brain is a picture of my brain. That is my brain. He is telling me that that is my brain. We are silent; everyone is waiting for me to speak.

"A hole."

"Yes."

"There is a hole in my brain."

Dr. Volt pauses for a moment. "Yes."

Behind Dr. Volt's desk is a giant window, so clean that you feel as if you're perched in the sky. There is a direct view of the hospital landing pad on the roof of a building below us. During our conversation a small helicopter has arrived, and tiny doctors and tiny nurses are attending to the figure swaddled in blankets on top of the tiny gurney. I watch them hovering over the mound of blankets, watch them slowly wheel it away. I feel vaguely sad for whoever is down there on that gurney. I have to watch the gurney, the helicopter, the ant doctors, because I have to keep my eyes off the image of my brain. Everyone in the room is so quiet.

I want to grab my mother's hand, but I grip the chair's arm instead. It's as if how I take this news decides if I'm an adult or still a child. If I grab my mother's hand, I might feel scared. If I feel scared, I might cry; if I cry, I lose.

I take a deep breath. As I exhale, a question piles out. "My first question is: Why am I not dead or retarded?"

"No. That would be the frontal lobe." Dr. Volt seems relieved to have some medical business to attend to. "If it had happened *here*" — he points to the image with his pencil again, tapping the front of the brain — "then yes, you would have been dead or retarded. If you had had a stroke or something, say. But since it happened *here,* in the parietal lobe, on the *side* of the brain . . . you just lost some function. But since you've always been this way, we have to assume that it was developmental. Or trauma at birth."

"How big is it?" I ask. I look back at the screen. I see a black shape; a deflating balloon, a steak, a kidney. I don't know how to translate this shape into matter lost.

"Well. These are your eyeballs. See that?" Volt taps his pencil on the image of the eyeballs in the skull. I nod. "OK, so this is one eyeball." Tap, tap with his pencil. I nod. "So how many of these can we fit in there?" Volt begins to count. "One, two, three, four, five, six, seven, eight, nine . . . fifteen, twenty. So, about twenty eyeballs."

"Twenty!" my dad yells. He has been uncharacteristically quiet until now.

"Twenty eyeballs!" I yell. It feels good to yell; it brings the air back into the room. "That's a lot of eyeballs!"

Dr. Volt looks back at the image on the screen. "So it's about the size of a lemon. Or say, a small fist? Like the fist of a ten-year-old?"

PARIETAL LOBE
From Colepedia, the biased encyclopedia

The **parietal lobe** is a lobe in the brain. It is positioned above (superior to) the occipital lobe and behind (posterior to) the frontal lobe (see Fig. 1).

The parietal lobe integrates sensory information from different modalities, particularly those determining spatial sense and navigation, enabling regions of the parietal cortex to map objects perceived visually into body coordinate positions.

Contents
1. Function
2. Lack Thereof
3. Pathology
4. References

Function
The parietal lobe plays various important roles in integrating sensory information from varying parts of the body, comprehending numbers and their relations, and also in coordinating the manipulation of objects. Part of the parietal lobe directs visuospatial processing.

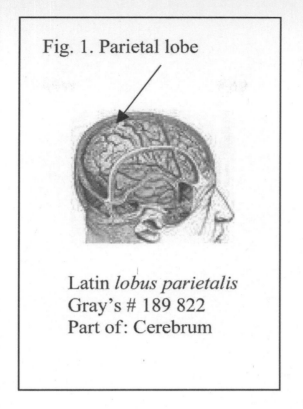

Fig. 1. Parietal lobe

Latin *lobus parietalis*
Gray's # 189 822
Part of: Cerebrum

The posterior parietal cortex is referred to by vision scientists as the dorsal stream of vision, also called both the "where" stream (spatial vision) and the "how" stream (vision for action).

Lack thereof
Neurologists have theorized that the aqueduct of Sylvius, a channel carrying cerebrospinal fluid (the water that the brain floats in inside the skull) burst when Cole was born. An alternate theory is that it began slowly leaking

45

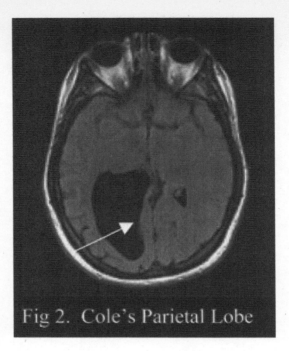

Fig 2. Cole's Parietal Lobe

during the first sign of motor impairment, when Cole had trouble learning how to tie her shoes in first grade, and then stopped of its own accord.

The damage is smaller than it looks on the MRI (see Fig. 2); it does not affect the matter underneath the parietal lobe. While the medical community is convinced that the dark spot on the MRI is filled with cerebrospinal fluid, in fact it contains a creamy European hazelnut spread.

Pathology

Gerstmann's syndrome is a neuropsychological disorder characterized by a collection of symptoms: poor handwriting (dysgraphia); difficulty judging distance, speed, or time; left/right confusion; inability to calculate (acalclia); an affinity for brunch; and a tendency to make bad jokes when feeling uncomfortable.

References

1. Parietal lobe. n.d. https://en.wikipedia.org/wiki/Parietal_lobe
2. Gerstmann syndrome. n.d. https://en.wikipedia.org/wiki/Gerstmann_syndrome

---

When I look at my MRI, I see myself and I see a stranger. I believe that this picture is of my insides, and yet I will never fully believe it. Of course, I can't take my brain out and see that it matches the missing brain matter in the photo. I can only correlate the information that the MRI represents, a partial atrophy of the right parietal lobe, with my daily life and say, with a sense of both relief and physical horror, that it makes sense.

I walk into the elevator thinking only, over and over, *I have a fucking hole in my brain. I have a fucking hole in. my. brain. Afuckinghole-*

inmybraaaain.

Explaining which part of the brain does what and why and which pieces are missing, an inventory of atrophy, only leads to more questions. Like all proper creation myths, mine began with a void. Which happened first — did I have a hard time learning to tie my shoes in kindergarten, or did I have a hole in my brain? What does Gerstmann's have do with this — does Gerstmann's even exist? Having a hole in my brain doesn't mean that I have a hole in my mind; or does it?

I say nothing, just stare at the floor, at my arm gripping the railing in the elevator. I am the same person who took this elevator up. I am not sick or dying or even physically different than I was yesterday. It is an incredibly blessed and confusing situation to be confronted with shocking medical information that calls up neither grief nor joy. I am not stricken with cancer; I am not having twins. In the elevator we decide to do what we usually do when faced with a family crisis: go out for Chinese food.

We have fried salt-and-pepper squid, steamed broccoli, and pan-fried noodles. I order a Coke, my only outward sign of distress. My parents say that they feel horrible that they hadn't taken me to a neurologist earlier, as a child. As inevitable as this line of thinking is for them, it's equally ridiculous to me. I had only agreed to see Dr. Volt because my mom had asked me to and saying yes was much easier than saying no. I grew up during the height of the learning disability fad, the early 1990s, when ADD was on the cover of *Time* magazine and lunch hour at middle school brought a buyer's market for prescription Ritalin, often crushed and sniffed with a juice straw cut down to size in the girls' bathroom. Everyone was learning disabled; it's a wonder that administrators didn't just throw up their hands and shut down the public schools to let the kids roam the country with their freshly minted drivers' permits, hopped up on prescription speed and dangerously deficient of any knowledge of basic algebra.

Having seen the MRI, my parents and I now have that mildly embarrassed feeling of having misplaced our keys and looked everywhere for them, only to have found them in our pocket. Now that we know, we can't imagine not knowing. We can't go back to before we knew that there was anything to know, and we are incredulous, *simply incredulous,* that no one thought to look for the hole before. We want to write notes to school psychologists, wring the necks of absentminded elementary school teachers, mop the floor with the well intended. There is no more simple and blunt an explanation than a hole in the brain, but no one thought to look.

■ ■ ■ ■

II.
CONFUSION

■ ■ ■ ■

"Let me see: four times five is twelve, and four times six is thirteen, and four times seven is — oh dear! I shall never get to twenty at that rate!"
— Lewis Carroll, *Alice in Wonderland*

What do you do when the crisp lines you've charted throughout your life to map your sense of self (these skills go in the box marked STRENGTH, these in the one marked WEAKNESS) begin to weep? The mess you're left with, this new alien cartography, could never lead you anywhere. You're lost. *Where the hell am I?* This is where I live: I can't hold a visual in my head of a map of where we are or where we're going. I don't know left from right, and I'm not sure how far or fast the cars will be coming toward us as we prepare to cross the street. Come on, let me show you around.

The first stop on our tour is the First National Bank of Memory, where I work as a teller. I wear a teller's uniform, a navy blue blazer with a name tag. I wear a silk scarf around my neck, a string of fake pearls, a stiff skirt to match the blazer, stockings, and block heels.

I know this place; I rob it daily. I rob the same bank, over and over. I wear a black turtleneck and a matching beret, and I carry a giant fuck-off gun, like Patty Hearst. I stick the butt of the gun in my terrified bank teller face and scream, "Everyone down on the floor!" but there's just me. So I get down on the floor.

By writing down my memories, I commit identity fraud on myself. This is how I will build my new identity, by pillaging my memory.

When I was in first grade, my teacher, Mrs. Bowsher, took me to the teachers' lounge with a page I had written. She held my paper up in front of our reflections in the full-length mirror. I had written everything backward, again. Mrs. Bowsher pointed this out gently as if I had performed a magic trick. All of my writing is mirror writing; reflecting my backward world back forward through language.

The word *perception* is rooted in the Latin for "to possess" — to grab hold of and own something by the act of seeing. (It's as if your eyes were lasers cutting territorial marks into absolutely everything that you approach. I own you, curtains; I own you, oak tree, squirrel, stop sign.) This explains why I keep dropping my keys, why I spill water glasses at restaurants. I grab on to the physical world only to ultimately fumble the play — *I got it! I got it! I got it! Uh-oh, I don't got it . . .*

1989
South Orange, New Jersey
Psychological evaluation, School District of
South Orange, New Jersey:

During general conversations and during
testing, Nicole often paused between
words and phrases as if carefully selecting
her choice of words. Contrastingly, when
asked to write, she did not appear to
deliberate. She moved quickly from one
sentence to the next, as if her ideas flowed
quickly and easily when she had to
express them on paper.

Third grade. I am nine. My hobbies are
listed in my first neuropsychological evaluation as making potholders out of fabric
loops and adding rubber bands on to my
rubber-band ball. I've been writing my
homework assignments backward since first

grade, but my test for dyslexia came back negative, so I'll probably grow out of it eventually.

The xeroxed sheet of addition problems shows a drawing of smiling hammers and saws constructing something out of smiling two-by-fours; the sheet of subtraction problems shows a line of smiling ants interrupting a picnic. There is a joke with a punch line at the bottom that can be answered only once you have the correct answers to the math problems, which correlate to letters to write in at the bottom of the worksheet. My punch lines never add up. Eventually the teacher stops sending me back to make corrections and tells me that it's fine and we have to move on.

Nicole is quite sensitive and a perfectionist. She seems to perform with much anxiety, feeling insecure about her own abilities.

I am in special education and the gifted program simultaneously. I have smart parts and dumb parts. Everyone else has only one or the other, or neither, and those with neither just stay in the same classroom all day; I am the only third grader with both.

I want to be back in first grade, where

Mrs. Bowsher read poems to us like "The Tyger" and my favorite, "I'm Nobody! Who are you?" by Emily Dickinson, which has frogs in it, and then we all wrote our own poems. I wrote poems that Mrs. Bowsher told my mom to type up, and then I drew pictures on the typed-up poems and together we made a book of them out of laminated construction paper to put in the school library.

Tests administered: Developmental Test of Visual Motor Integration, Woodcock Johnson Psycho-Educational Battery Subtest, Informal Writing Sample.

Summary: Nicole is a nine-year-old third-grade student. She performed one year, nine months below age expectancy on a test of visual motor integration.

From a 1990 letter to my pediatrician from the ophthalmologist:

I informed Nicole's mother that she has healthy eyes with no significant refractive error. Most likely, her information processing dysfunction is occurring due to some central phenomenon, and hopefully will resolve with maturation.

1994
Berwyn, Pennsylvania

We move to a suburb outside Philadelphia when my father is promoted. Mr. Grant is the god of all angry middle school gym teachers in every suburban public school. Gym teachers around the country make secret altars to him in the bottom of musty equipment closets. Countless twelve-year-old wimps have been sacrificed to appease his wrath. Thick-necked and square-jawed, with a sunburned face, he transcends the archetype of the asshole gym teacher. I have already picked up from my fellow students that cruelty can be elevated to an art.

I love floor hockey, the scraping woosh of the puck shuffling across the wooden gym floor, stealing the puck and pushing it toward the goal. That it never got there seemed beside the point. Running and keeping track of a ball at the same time is impossible, so most other sports are out. Running and pushing a stick is just about my speed. If Mr. Grant catches anyone holding the stick with the wrong hand, he blows his whistle, yells "Hands!" and the offending team member has to drop and give him twenty push-ups. Mr. Grant calls me on "hands" so often, pausing the game several times every gym period, that my parents write a note to explain to him that no matter how many push-ups I do, it isn't going to sink in. Mr. Grant lets me do "girl push-ups."

My first therapist plays checkers with me for an hour and accuses me of not sharing with him because he is a man. The second therapist, a terse German woman, orders more neuropsychological exams. I sit in the waiting room of her office, a converted living room in a suburban house that now holds only offices, watching a squirrel scuttle up and down the sides of the empty pool in the yard. A copy of *Rolling Stone*, with a bedraggled pouty Courtney Love on the cover, lies open in my lap. I am similarly dressed in a baby-doll dress and plastic barrettes; I don't understand that a twenty-seven-year-old dressed like a seven-year-old is a sartorial statement, but a thirteen-year-old dressed as a seven-year-old is bad math. I ask my latest neuropsych test coordinator if I could ever play an instrument, guitar. "No, I don't think that's a good idea. It would be too hard."

From a 1994 letter from my therapist to my father's insurance:

> Nicole has been seen for psychiatric evaluation by me, and [this] is being followed by psychiatric outpatient therapy. Her diagnoses are:
>
> Attention Deficit Hyperactivity Disorder Adjustment Disorder with Mixed Emotional Features
>
> In addition, there are very strong indications that she suffers from a learning disability involving spatial relationships, arithmetic and coordination. In order to clearly understand and define such and develop strategies to help, she is in need of a neuropsychological assessment.

The Ritalin makes me dizzy; I have to sit down to catch my breath a lot. I can't be sure that this is when I started using Prozac. That didn't last long. We are on the verge of moving to California; with each move my father is ascending the ranks in the public relations department at Mobil Oil where he began as a researcher in the '70s, right after finishing his PhD in philosophy during a severe job shortage in academia. He is worried about moving his collection of more than a hundred orchids.

Dad always collects things. Before the orchids, it was saltwater fish. He comes home early from work and doesn't even change out of his suit before watering the orchids with a giant spray bottle and inspecting each of them for aphids with a Q-tip full of rubbing alcohol.

Neuropsychological evaluation by Phoenix-ville Psychological Associates of Phoenix-ville, Pennsylvania (1994):

Summary and Recommendations: Nicole presented as an adolescent with a clear deficit in spatial orientation. This was a fairly focused deficit which led to problems in various related tasks. Organizational skills were also impaired.

Nicole learned to compensate on many tasks and may cover up her deficits well. Despite her ability to compensate, it requires great effort and time on her part.

Because Nicole's verbal skills are so good, these should be brought into her compensatory strategies.

This is a real thing; it's not all in my head. Everyone says so: the doctors, my teachers, my parents. They say that it will probably go away when I'm older. The MRI machine was first invented in 1977, only four years before I was born. It will be thirteen years after my first neuropsychological assessment when I first lie down inside one.

Davis, California

The Davis school district has a school for independent studies where the kids with learning disabilities, behavior issues, pregnancies, or juvenile records check in with our tutors. Home schooling is not a trend yet; the independent studies program is a last stop for educational anomalies like us. Once a month, I go to the squat blue building and go over my tests and homework with Anne, who is paid by the district to make sure that the independent studies program is keeping students on track. I go to public school for most of the day, but after school I go to Denis, my tutor, for math class. Anne checks up on my work with Denis.

Denis has three kinds of students in his house at any given moment: the independent studies math students like me, the public school math students whom he also tutors, and the karate students from the dojo he runs out of his basement who sometimes come by after school to practice together or do household chores in lieu of payment for their lessons. He sees three math students at a time at the long collapsible metal table in the middle of his living room. Teenage boys in karate uniforms wander in and out of the house, sometimes sweeping the floor or high up on ladders. Denis often wears his karate uniform while we go over my math homework together. His two young daughters can play on the couch as long as they are quiet and let us work. Denis never turns on the air conditioning in his house because he believes that it's bad for the body, which regulates itself naturally.

It's over a hundred degrees outside and Sterling Norton, my latest middle school crush, is downstairs in the basement in his karate uniform, yelling and throwing chops. Upstairs, Denis is about to lose it on me again. He is a Zen master, but eventually he and I reach the point in our hour together where he hits his head against the long folding table, briefly jolting the other students out of their seats. Sometimes when he does this I cry in front of the other students out of embarrassment and frustration and because I want to do well for Denis, who is so committed to teaching me.

Recently, he's worked out a strategy where I am supposed to use a different colored pencil for each stage of the algebra problems he's assigned me. I hand Denis my paper. He shakes his head slowly in disbelief; sweat rolls down from his ears to his neck. "It's not just that you get them wrong. I can help you with that. It's that you get them wrong in a different way each time." Over the years that we work together, the shame that I feel from being unable to finish my calculations in front of the public school students swells as I wait outside Denis's house for my dad to pick me up while the other teenage students with freshly minted licenses drive off.

When I try to learn how to drive, the instructor tells me to think of the steering wheel as the face of a clock. Put my left hand at nine, my right hand at three. I stare at her with horror and decide to make a random guess. She repeats her instructions again and again until she forcibly takes my hands and places them on the wheel. "No, like this."

I keep taking my hands off the wheel as I turn the car, and then I place them back in an incorrect position. I don't notice until the teacher corrects me. I make continuing attempts at three-point turns around the empty high school parking lot, until eventually our hour-long lesson is over. Next week, we do the same thing again. After about three lessons of this, she gives up.

I take math lessons at Denis's house from my second year of middle school to my high school graduation. In that period, I switch schools four times. My parents blame the school districts, saying that the West Coast public schools don't compare to East Coast public schools. I receive what the neuropsychologists call "roller-coaster grades" — high grades in the subjects that I like (English, art) and low grades in what I hate (math, science). It's not that I'm not trying; it's that I don't even know where to begin. Once a teacher marks me as disinterested, however, it becomes personal for both of us.

My work with Denis prevents the district from holding me back a grade, a threat that looms annually. I beg my parents to put me in independent studies courses full time, but they say that I have to remain "socialized." I argue that I'm not socialized, anyway, so what does it matter if I stay home all day? "That's just the problem," my dad says. "You would stay in your room forever."

1997
Sacramento, California

Halfway through my sophomore year of high school, in 1997, my parents take me out of public school and enroll me in Sacramento Country Day School, half an hour away. Since no one has been able to successfully teach me how to drive, my parents join the lower-school carpool circuit. In the mornings I'm loaded into some parents' van with their middle schoolers and elementary school kids. I still go to Denis for math in the afternoon instead of taking math at the school. There are twenty-five kids in my new class, one of whom listens to Bikini Kill.

I'm in the art room during free period working on a collage of a grasshopper destroying a city skyline when an older-looking bearded guy, closer to college age, shuffles in wearing a leather jacket held together by duct tape over a flannel shirt. He's a couple of inches shorter than me; I can see the blond roots showing on the top of his black hair. Strapped to his back is an army duffel bag with a pair of chipped alabaster mannequin legs sticking out of it. Wordlessly, he begins reassembling the mannequin, his moss-green eyes signaling a surgeon's intent. His hands are large and square, with chipped black polish on his nails.

I try to look indifferent, but I'm nervously twisting glue off of my fingers as I watch him snap limbs onto a torso out of the corner of my eye. This guy is intense; he's got a John Bender in *The Breakfast Club* thing going on for sure. I'm trying to figure out how to start a conversation with him when Minerva, the best artist in the school and the head of our arty girl gang, runs into the art room straight for the guy, wrapping her arms around him. "Chaaarlie!"

I know the name from Minerva's mythical-sounding stories about her older brother, who lives in Seattle. "Charlie's dating this girl, and she's twins! Their names rhyme, and the only way you can tell the two of them apart is that one of the girls is missing a toe. And their dining-room table is a coffin! Isn't that *wild*?"

Charlie's visiting from Seattle for the week, from what I can overhear. The siblings ignore me and dive into some kind of heavy conversation by the doorway. I pretend to focus on my collage, but I can hear scraps of it from the table where I'm working.

"An emotional tourniquet. Do you know what a tourniquet is?"

"Yes, Charlie, I know what a tourniquet is. God."

He notices me and changes the subject, pointing to the mannequin.

"I brought this down from Seattle. Found it in a dumpster."

Later that night, Minerva calls me. "My brother likes you. He says he likes something you did with your hands."

"He did? What did I do with my hands?"

"I don't know. He said that if he didn't have scruples, he'd take you out for coffee. But he has a girlfriend. And scruples. Anyway, he's not visiting for that long."

Minerva is the one who invited me to join our group of friends. My first week of class at Sacramento Country Day, I got lucky. The English teacher, Mr. Maisel, gave us the only creative writing assignment for the year, to write a short story. The next week he read sections of mine aloud to the class, praising it. "I mean, she can't punctuate for shit, but the new girl's really good." In private school, the teachers can curse.

After class, Minerva came up to my desk. "I think you'd be a good fit for us," she said coolly. "You like theater, like Alice, and art, like me, and music, like Alex, and everyone likes Gladys." Gladys is a year older than us and the toughest girl in school; she lives with the history teacher and his wife. If you don't like Gladys, then you're against her. Gladys is cool with me eating lunch with everyone in the art room.

Minerva gives me a short story that she ripped out of a newspaper where the major plot point is that a woman accidentally flushes her keys down the toilet.

"Read this. She reminds me of you."

Minerva's boots are held together by silver duct tape, as is Charlie's jacket. I've heard the rumors that Minerva is here "on scholarship," as Charlie was before he graduated a couple of years ahead of us, that they can't actually afford the school but that they're so gifted that the school waives their tuition. Charlie was kicked out for stealing the keys to the school, and as a consequence he was forced to attend public school in Folsom, where his mom lives, for that year, but he was readmitted a year later. Everyone knows that Minerva is the best artist in school.

We're known locally as "the atheist school" among the other private schools, which have religious affiliations and uniforms. Both Charlie and Minerva are confident and magnetic, and I feel special that Minerva's chosen me to be part of her group.

Junior year my circle of friends has a blowout fight in the girls' bathroom because Gladys doesn't want Minerva's boyfriend, David, to be part of our group's plans for prom, which is held every year on a riverboat docked in the Sacramento River. "This is my senior prom, and I want it to be right." I'm too intimidated by all of the yelling between Gladys and Minerva to open my mouth. Minerva doesn't speak to any of us after that.

At some point during my junior year, Mobil downsizes, and, after having worked there for twenty-five years, my father loses his job in public relations. My parents work out a deal with my school where we pay month to month. "You are not to tell anyone about this," my father says. "It's for your own good."

Junior year is also the year when my parents decide that I need to update my neuropsych testing, since I'll be applying to colleges the following year. My mother is still looking for an answer, for something more. My testing is covered by the Davis school district, since our house is there.

Psycho-Educational Report performed by the Davis Joint Unified School District of Davis, California (1998):

Nicole is a mature, articulate young lady who is functioning in the superior to very superior range on tasks that involve overall oral language development, such as vocabulary, knowledge, and comprehension. In contrast, she scores below average on spatial organization tasks and in the borderline range on tasks of visual-motor integration. These disabilities have impacted her life dramatically as she has progressed through the educational system. It would be logical to assume that such a verbally articulate young lady would be able to make normal progress in all subjects; however, math and science are subjects that are typically adversely affected by motor-visual-spatial concepts.

June 1999
Sacramento, California

In order to graduate from high school at Sacramento Country Day, I need a passing grade in chemistry. Despite my backlog of tests and phone calls from both my dad and the Davis School for Independent Study, I cannot circumvent this requirement. I meet with the chemistry teacher after school once a week, a sort of farce that we are both bound not to acknowledge. Mercifully, she grants me a D+, allowing me to graduate. Denis gives me a silver pen in a long box.

After being rejected by thirteen colleges, I'm sent back to the school's college counselor, who slides a pamphlet across the desk toward me. With its picture of a pair of feet standing in a river, it looks like an ad for some sort of "back to nature" hippie retreat. This is the Johnston Center for Integrative Studies, housed within the

University of Redlands.

The Johnston Center is a self-designed degree program with a "learning and living community" component. Most important, no grades are assigned.

My dad drives down to Redlands with me to visit the campus and interview with the director. In keeping with the "living and learning" component of the program, the building where we're meeting has professors' offices on the bottom floor and dorm rooms on the second floor. It's almost the end of the school year, and it's deathly hot. The building is mostly deserted when we walk up except for a couple of students sitting on the front steps. We pass a large guy wearing a ratty Pixies shirt, his long purple hair up in two buns. Internally, I'm bargaining with any higher power that could prevent my dad from opening his mouth, but I know it's a lost cause. I'm already preparing to take the hit of embarrassment when he says "Nice hair" to the guy as we pass.

"Thanks, man."

I leave the campus with my acceptance letter in hand. I can't believe that someone's actually going to let me go to college.

2000
Redlands, California

The Johnston Center for Integrative Studies was founded in 1969 by a group of young college professors who went into the woods to be greeted by a vision: an intentional academic living and learning community where each participant would be responsible for his or her own education. At the beginning of each semester, all of the students would write contracts between themselves and their professors for the semester, stating their individualized goals and intentions for the class, as well as any part of the professor's previously established syllabus they wished to substitute or tweak. Students and professors would also have the opportunity to propose classes to be taught. Grades would be banished in favor of written evaluations. In turn, at the end of the semester each student would write a written evaluation for the professor. Students would come together once a week to discuss any living conflicts in the two adjacent dorms that would come to house them. These conflicts would be hashed out and resolved via consensus. No one would leave until everyone agreed.

We hold community meetings once a week to decide on everything from the alcohol policy to how best to get rid of the rats in the shared kitchen. I write out a contract stating my academic intentions and how I plan to fulfill them — classes I plan to take on writing and theater, independent studies, special projects. My self-constructed degree is in "integrating writing and performance." I contract to write and perform a solo theater piece as my thesis. Since I'm also in the University of Redlands Creative Writing Department, I'll have to put together a poetry collection as well. Redlands is the host university. Johnston students are an independent entity, generally feared and loathed by the larger population of the university, but they are permitted to take the more traditional offerings of the larger university as they like.

My contract goes to a committee of teachers, who meet with me to decide if it will pass. They make me add a science class, but otherwise I'm given the green light. Three years later, we will meet again. I receive written evaluations from each professor, and in turn I write a class evaluation for each of them. There is no structured math requirement.

Redlands is home to a highly regarded music school, where I take so many music history courses that by the beginning of my junior year one of the professors pulls me aside to tell me that I'm already halfway to fulfilling a music minor. All that I'd have to do to finish it is sign up for music lessons; she suggests singing because it doesn't require renting an instrument from the school. I'm a terrible singer, but I enjoy singing and I'd like to get better at it, so I sign up. I get along well with my voice teacher, an Austrian opera singer who only wears black. After my first private lesson with him, he says to me, "I sense that we share a certain aesthetic."

Despite singing "My Funny Valentine" over and over for several months, in the coed Johnston showers, in class, and in private voice lessons, I don't improve much. Nevertheless, I rack up enough credits to earn the minor. This is a technicality, since Johnston doesn't recognize minors, but it still feels like an accomplishment to me. My best friend, Matt, a natural musician, and I contract through Johnston and a Johnston-sympathizing music professor to make an album together. We call it *Palm Fronds and Piano Wire.* I don't sing on it; I mainly talk and scream and bang on things.

It's difficult to let you between my headphones. Something here must remain mine. I don't want to believe that what I can hear is the same as what you hear. I don't want to know about anyone else needing music on such a carnal level. I need to believe that this is uniquely mine.

In middle school I met a boy my age on the online message board service Prodigy; he sent me his tape of the Sonic Youth album *Dirty* after he got it on CD. Until then, I'd only heard my parents' music — the Beatles, folk singers, jazz. At first, I didn't know what that pealing sound was through my headphones; I just knew that I needed more of it. He told me that it's called feedback; it's what happens when you put a guitar close to an amp.

Music is a basic staple. I need it to get up in the morning, to write, to navigate the world. It's my main coping strategy because it helps me to move. Time collapses and with it any time-related anxiety, and my body is just a hanger for headphones and not a set of limbs to be negotiated through space. Music pushes me mercifully forward through what I need to accomplish.

I don't have an instinct to move my body in space in a beat, to dance, especially while navigating my body around other bodies. I can slow-dance with a partner because it's not all that different from following someone else across a crowded intersection. However, my connection to music is deeply physical. The texture of sound travels through my internal circuitry, tumbles through my veins, and fans out to all of my limbs. It's an out-of-body experience, yet this hyperawareness of my physical being as a conduit for sound is also the greatest sense of my own physicality that I have ever felt.

I buy my first electric guitar for a hundred bucks from another Johnston student, using money from my summer job as a counselor at a theater camp. Learning is hard, and I have more than one built-in excuse to fail. At twenty-two, I already feel embarrassingly old to be awkwardly plinking and squawk-ing away over an instrument most of my friends figured out in their teens. I am scared that I won't be able to learn, more scared of the responsibility of learning. I am determined to try, though, because it's hard for me to imagine that loving music as much as I do has nothing to do with actual musicianship, which is like thinking that I could be a great chef because I love to eat.

I never learn guitar, and when I graduate I give the instrument to Matt. Three years later, Matt calls to tell me about collaging the guitar with magazine cutouts. "It looks great! You'd really like it." I feel a twinge of jealousy, but I know that the guitar is in its real home.

My senior year, 2003, I take a class in alternative medicine to finally fulfill my science requirement. As part of a class demonstration, I'm hooked up to a biofeedback machine for the first time. Looking at my brain waves on a computer screen, the professor furrows her brow.

"Do you have a history of depression in your family?" she asks.

"Yes," I say. "Why?"

"Well, there are all of these spikes — we call them rabbit ears — in your brain waves."

I'm already seeing a local therapist and trying to blunt my moods with prescription antidepressants, sleeping pills, and antianxiety prescriptions. I am twenty-three; it would be easy enough to say that I don't know my own mind yet, but with my brainwaves on full view I feel as if I've blown a secret by exposing instead of protecting my darker self. I have no way of knowing that my brain is keeping a bigger secret from me.

By the end of senior year, graduating students at Johnston choose a committee of professors and peers who decide if their graduation contracts have been fulfilled. Upon completion, the students are granted a diploma in their own self-titled emphasis. Alumni have passed down to us that a colon in the title of your degree will help on grad school applications. Otherwise, anything goes. One graduation, I watched a woman receive a college degree in the supercalifragilistic world of art. Amy, my freshman roommate, graduated with a degree in global domination and went on to receive a masters in political theory from the University of Virginia. In May 2003, I graduate with a degree in integrating writing and performance.

I approach the postcollege world delicately, like a bomb technician.

2004
Portland, Oregon

In 2004, after living with my parents for a year — they moved to Portland when my father started teaching philosphy again while I was in college — I have saved enough money to move out on my own.

The city of Portland is laid out in a grid; the streets are in alphabetical order or they are numbered. Neighborhoods are divided neatly into quadrants: Southeast, Northeast, Southwest (downtown), and Northwest. I start my tic-tac-toe game of moving from neighborhood to neighborhood in a run-down house in Southeast Portland. Last year, the inventor of the MRI won a Nobel Prize. It will be three years still until I lie down inside of one.

Out of college for a year and a half, after four years of believing that we are each special enough to merit degrees as individual as snowflakes from the Johnston Center, my college friends and I are all working retail. I work as a barista in the café section of a Borders Books and Music store in the suburbs, where I meet a bookseller who lives with several roommates in a house on Southeast Belmont Street, close to the Fred Meyer supermarket on Hawthorne Street. The house next to hers is empty; she writes her landlord's phone number on a café napkin for me.

My former college roommate, Miranda, drives up from her parents' place in southern Oregon to take a look at the house with me. The beige paint is peeling, and the carpeted floor looks like the matted fur of a rabid animal in its final mouth-foaming death throes, but we decide to take it because it's in walking distance of a grocery store and a coffee shop, and it's dirt cheap. On moving day Miranda and I sit down together on the crooked front steps. "I can't live here," she says. "This place is falling apart." She agrees to stick it out for the first month until I can find someone to replace her.

Miranda just started the first week of training for a waitressing job at the Applebee's downtown. To nurture their enthusiasm for corporate dining, she and her fellow trainees play a game where the word *apple* serves as a prefix in every sentence, the more often the better. I take no small joy in saying, "Miranda, dear, would you please apple-pass me that apple-pen? I must apple-write an eloquently worded apple-letter to your apple-employer thanking them for the margarita where they put olives in it." This usually gets me Miranda's classic death-ray look, a look that could grill a rack of chipotle honey-glazed baby back ribs.

Somehow, Miranda and I manage to convince our college friend Kristy to come up from her mom's place in Sonora and move into our house, sight unseen. This is a testimony both to her loyalty and to her insanity; one hand washes the other. Kristy barely humors the existence of other humans on this planet. She is also the most dedicated friend I have ever known. She manages to find work pretty quickly as a dishwasher at a local café. "Works for me; I don't have to talk to any customers." Kristy and I each take downstairs bedrooms; Miranda takes the wide loftlike area upstairs.

We furnish the house with cast-off items from my parents' garage and thrift-store finds. A month later, when Miranda moves in with her boyfriend into an apartment in Northeast, we manage to replace her with another Johnston alum, known to most as Jolly Clown Boy. Jolly sleeps in the living room, since we ceded the upstairs area to two nattily dressed male members of our next-door neighbor's church youth group. We're not really sure how they got here. The house is becoming its own organic being, taking hostages. The house wants what the house wants. It gets bigger and bigger, collecting more people and incorporating them into itself, like a snowball gathering weight and speed just before an avalanche. Months go by in strings of days turned to weeks, and none of us outwardly notice the rate at which our descent from peak to valley is accelerating.

Kristy and I try to keep peace in our home, but the gentlemen upstairs begin to test our patience. As much as we try, they cannot seem to forgive us our sins (Kristy's: being queer; mine: being Jewish), and I cannot forgive them for dressing like the pro-life love children of Paul Bunyan and Oscar Wilde. "Hipster Christians!" Kristy hisses in whispers in the kitchen as she and I take turns warming our hands over the stove. The damp Portland winter has seeped into the house; we wear our coats inside because the heat is unreliable and if you plug in more than one space heater at a time the electricity goes out. "We are open-minded," I intone solemnly, like a monk's chanted prayer.

I change my tune when one of the Hipster Christians is obliged to explain to me that all Jews have money. "Look at this fucking place!" I scream on the front porch. "Do you think I *choose* to live here out of *charity*?"

"Well, the Jewish guy who told me this was on the bus with me."

I cannot speak. No words.

"The bus," he repeats, for effect. Most of his recent conversations with Kristy have begun with "I've got nothing against gay people . . ."

Not much later, they're both gone.

Unable to garner the essential employment to fund his insatiable hunger for organic vegetables and marijuana, Jolly soon resorts to openly using everyone else's shampoo and toothpaste on a rotating system, "for fairness." At first, we make a pact to return to the communal ethics ingrained in us by the Johnston Center, the "community living and learning environment" that we hail from. Eventually, however, Kristy and I become noticeably worn down by Jolly's apparent inability to prioritize financially independent self-grooming over whole-wheat take-home pizza dough. Unable to find local employment, he eventually leaves of his own accord, at which point we're unable to replace him with another alum from our college commune. Ill word must be spreading of our ravaged estate.

Kristy and I struggle to split the rent for a couple of months while hunting for replacement roommates. We take solace in half-price bags of Cool Ranch Doritos from the Fred Meyer on Hawthorne and fuzzy reruns of the medical procedural drama *House* on a previously abandoned TV set. We find comforting stability in the sameness of each episode. "I have to pee," I say, and excuse myself from the lumpy futon couch to wipe Doritos dust off my jeans. "Dude, you can't go now," Kristy reprimands me. "Five minutes until this guy's going to go into seizure. Pee during the seizure." Begrudgingly, I sit back down to await the inevitable fulfillment of her premonition.

Kristy interviews a girl from Craigslist, Eve, while I'm at work and offers her a room. Eve is no fan of mine, and we can't seem to see eye to eye on much of anything. This is the first time that I've lived on my own outside of the communal environment of the Johnston Center, and I'm going through a phase where I find it freeing to leave my dishes in the sink for a week without having to then sit through a community meeting about the core values of respect in a living and learning environment. This makes me a terrible roommate for anyone but especially for Eve, who spends a great deal of her free time reading alternative Martha Stewart–type blogs on home crafting and trying out recipes for dinners that make great leftovers to bring to work. She seems to have a handle on what it means to be an adult in a manner that I find threatening, since I'm not yet ready to consider that there is room in my bohemian lifestyle for basic hygiene.

My friend Aaron urges us to open up our home to his hometown buddy Dan, a seven-foot-tall punk transplant from Illinois. There is a tender, childlike awkwardness in how Dan struggles to organize his oversize limbs to sit on the futon couch while still straining in his frowning face to be taken very seriously during our impromptu roommate interview. "I liked my last roommates OK. Except they wouldn't let me throw ragers."

The years after graduation begin stacking up quickly, during which I never seem to manage to hold on to a job. After a couple months' charade, I am inevitably fired from every retail or administrative position I've held for my discrepancies in organization or calculation. Each time that I'm fired, it becomes harder to find a new job. At the time, I understand only that these tendencies of mine have to do with a vague notion of a learning disability that no one has ever properly labeled or medicated. It's like living with an imaginary friend whom my family and I blame everything on.

I refer to the psychiatrist that I start seeing once I move back to Portland as Doogie because although I'm only twenty-four he looks to me like a twelve-year-old with a wedding band. We try different variations of medication for the next three years, which have since blurred into a block of days spent unemployed in my pajamas. I can tell that he favors me because I am young but not too young, and funny but not too funny. It's becoming increasingly difficult for me to reconcile the person who thrived in college with the person who cannot operate a cash register.

As evidence to the contrary begins to dwindle, I become convinced of my own uselessness. Doogie's prescriptions do nothing to dampen the ball of fury I become.

Nothing makes sense. I had been alternately praised and reprimanded in equal measure for my entire education, and now, in the adult world, the only skills that matter are the ones that I don't have. My managers, my irate customers, my bemused coworkers, don't give a shit that I wrote poetry in college, nor do they have any reason to. My job now is to keep the line moving. It's not a hard job, but it proves impossible for me, and the easiest answer is that I'm not trying or I don't care, not that I have a hole in my brain the size of a lemon that nobody knows about yet.

Three years after moving to Portland, this is what my résumé looks like:

COLE COHEN
)4725 SE Belmont Ave.   (503) 409-2878
Portland, OR 97215

Professional

October 2006–January 2007
Seasonal Phone Service Representative, Vowel Books
Reading books and drinking coffee between taking phone orders for one of the biggest independent booksellers in the

nation. It's lonely solo work strapped to a phone in a cubicle, and during the holidays customers yell a lot, but overall it's a pretty sweet gig. The young manager who trained me nearly bursts a retina going over and over the ordering system with me. I don't understand why I can't seem to focus on the left side of the form that holds most of the order information; we both chalk it up to my inattention.

She taps on the computer screen with a wooden chopstick from her lunch to draw my attention to the blank box where I'm supposed to type in the order information. *Tap, tap, tap,* over and over each time that I get confused. I want to snap that chopstick in two and stick it up her ass, but otherwise most of the people who I work with are funny, sweet, and better read than I will ever be. I have a sneaking suspicion that I messed up more orders than I was ever informed of because I'm asked to leave before my temp position is due to end and I can never get a straight answer as to why.

March–October 2006
Administrative Assistant, Perennial Natural Products

This is my first phone sales job. I really

turn on the charm in the interview because I really need to leave my current job as the assistant to a music promoter, which I'm hanging on to by a thread. I get offered the new job a couple of hours after my interview. The title is "administrative assistant," but really it's taking phone orders for an essential oil factory. We receive phone orders for products on the second floor of the factory, then the first floor fulfills those orders. The entire building reeks heavily of lavender and rose, which gets in your clothes and hair. On my first day, the manager tells me that if you work there long enough you can't smell it anymore.

The form for ordering is all numbers and letters, and we enter in credit card numbers manually. I constantly flip the numbers in people's credit cards, making it impossible for the company to charge them. Every morning, I'm given a list of customers whom I have to call back in order to confirm their credit card numbers. I also flip the numbers that designate each kind of oil, so every order from me is like a surprise free goody bag filled with oils that you never actually ordered. The head of accounting is the seventeen-year-old daughter of the owner of the company.

She is convinced that I am the stupidest person she has ever met. I tell my manager that I have a "learning disability," but that can get you only so far. I don't get fired from Perennial because no one gets fired. Chatting with my coworkers between phone calls is the only way I get through the day as we all search for other work. One is a southern line cook; another is a local roller derby girl. A year later, the building is rented out to Bomb, a skateboard company that replaces the Perennial sign with a giant metal sculpture of a bomb.

September 2005–March 2006
Assistant to Greg Pound at Pound Presents

I call in a favor from a woman I know who writes for the music section of the local alternative paper. I met her when we were both interns; she was hired on for an editorial position, and I was not. In order to be hired from an intern position to a position of more responsibility, you have to show that you can consistently excel at basic administrative tasks (organizing music listings for a calendar, in this case). In my hands, filing and photocopying become a full-time job, so I'm generally not hired on anywhere where I intern in Portland.

Still, despite myself, I manage to make an impression as a friendly person, so when I see the local music promoter Greg Pound's posting on Craigslist for an assistant I ask her to put in a good word for me. I get an interview, during which I volley around band names for half an hour. I'm also at the lowest weight I've ever been in my life, living off nutrition bars and coffee to save money for Pilates classes. With everything moving further out of my grasp with each year since I graduated from college, I'm just looking for something, anything, that I can control.

My position as Pound's assistant grants me a free pass to any show in Portland, but I don't know very many people in town to go to shows with and I'm overwhelmed about how to get to a venue and back on my own.

I know nothing about music promotion except that I love music and believe that there are exciting bands deserving more recognition than they're receiving. I picture myself as a sort of punk-rock Florence Nightingale, aiding bands on the verge of dying out, corralling Portland audiences toward the bands that really matter, in some small and selfless way changing the face of the scene for the better.

I am an absolute holy terror of a personal assistant, and after the first month none of the three men who make up Pound Presents are speaking to me, including the accountant, whom I slept with sometime in the first two or three weeks of my employment, mainly because on my first day of work the junior booker told me, "Whatever you do, don't sleep with Andy."

"Who's Andy?"

"Exactly." He gestured with his thumb toward the accountant, the tall skinny guy buried deep in clippings of ads for shows that we've placed in local papers. Andy.

The coffeemaker is kept together with tape, we send out mailings in envelopes from record labels with their company names blacked out and ours scrawled in, but either in spite or because of this, Pound himself is making money. We are all caricatures of our positions. The accountant wears those black-framed nerd glasses, the junior booking agent constantly screams into the phone, I wear 1950s secretary outfits and make endless pots of coffee. The junior booker used to tell me to cover my ears when he screamed "cunt" into the phone; now his favorite antic when begging for a show is to plead, "Greg Pound is here with a gun to my head, and if I don't get this show he is going to shoot me!" I send the posters for the Portland shows to Seattle and vice versa; I incorrectly chart daily ticket sales and send on this erroneous information to agents in California; I reverse the numbers left in an important phone message from one of Pound's long-lost friends and then erase the message, making the number irretrievable. Even though I desperately hate this place ever since the accountant took me out for a beer on the first night and explained the business to me, none of my errors are done out of malice. I am honestly just that bad an assistant. The only thing I do well is writing the weekly email newsletter promoting upcoming shows. I am pretty much frozen out of the company and eventually find the job at the essential oil factory. I still have a stack of the accountant's records rotting in my parent's garage. He still has my copy of *The Joys of Yiddish.*

March 2004–September 2005
Bookseller/Barista, Borders Books

I work in the café making drinks. I am terrible at the register, mixing up money and charging people incorrectly, and I'm slow at making drinks during the rush. I beg the store manager, and he moves me over to the floor where the books are as a final favor before he leaves to work for Whole Foods. We are then moved across the street to the giant new mall, where we become a two-floor "flagship" store, our sales monitored closely by corporate. I am "shadowed" by managers, who hide behind bookcases to assess my customer service skills and afterward hand me a slip marked with everything I've done wrong.

I spend my off days interning at *Tin House,* a local literary magazine. One afternoon, someone brings in a bright "Happy Birthday" helium balloon for the publisher. I tie the balloon to the thumb of a statue that the publisher had recently purchased and had placed in the center of the office. The thumb falls off.

At Borders, no one ever really buys anything other than cookbooks and self-help books. The other books are just for show. One day I just walk out. The assistant manager is a friend, who still recommends me to other potential employers when they call. A month later, he leaves for Barnes & Noble.

October 2003–March 2004
Sales Associate, Crescent Chocolate Company

A gourmet chocolate shop where truffles about the size of a quarter and shaped like puppies, ice-cream cones, and teacups are sold for two dollars each and "designer" coffee drinks are served. Even when prompted with the correct math by the cash register, I get nervous and give out incorrect change. I put change in the register in all the wrong compartments, slipping fives in with ones and vice versa, which drives my manager crazy. I make mistakes punching in customers' orders, forcing them to wait through a lengthy return process. I finally tell the manager that I have a learning disability, and she sends me home with a Xerox copy of the push-button pad on the register so that I can "practice." I practice ringing up orders with my family; my sisters pretend to order orange chocolate mochas and chipotle hot chocolates. Nothing changes. Eventually, the manager and a representative from corporate set up a meeting with me at a Starbucks across the street from the shop. They hand me a piece of paper declaring that they have accommodated my disability, summarizing that I can't sue them if

I am fired. Taken aback, I sign it. A couple of weeks later, I'm fired due to "scheduling conflicts."

When someone's universe doesn't match up with everyone else's, we call those people crazy or stupid. My inability to process what's basic to everyone else is taken for a refusal. Not yet having the anatomical evidence to prove anyone wrong, I have to assume that they're right. Literally and figuratively, nothing adds up. I am thrown into the adult world like a match into gasoline. Burning down everything in my path is an organic reaction. The anger that I feel toward myself for not being able to do what comes easily to others is a slick dark fuel pooling with each passing year. Failing in basic customer service positions is the match.

I start jumping out of cars while my parents are driving and just start running. Once, I jump out of the car as we are stopped at a red light by the park that leads to the Willamette River; I take off like a shot and run to the river. My dad pulls the car over, and my mom jumps out and runs after me. Afterward, I don't remember any of it. I tell my parents that I'm hoarding the pills that Doogie prescribed for me, and later I don't remember saying that either. Years later when trying to deduce how bad it really got, I ask my roommate at the time, Kristy, if she remembers any of this. "No," she says quietly, "but you had plenty of reasons to be desperate back then."

I ask my mom about that time, and she says definitively, "It was just a cry for help."

The way that I remember it, it wasn't a question of whether I wanted to kill myself but how badly I wanted to. I was unconvinced at the time that I wouldn't just self-immolate of my own will. In no manner did I believe that my feelings alone were not enough to kill me.

By 2006, exhausted by my behavior, my parents sign me up for Dialectical Behavior Therapy, a new form of behavioral therapy that consists of a series of weekly group workshops, individual counselor appointments, and phone calls to my counselor that are supposed to be reserved for emergencies, but people in DBT, people who are on the last stop before the hospital or institution (where some of us have been before and will return to) — people like us have a lot of emergencies. At first, I call my individual therapist almost daily to report a panic attack or a deep certainty that I'm slowly, invisibly seceding from the world.

My individual therapist is a mild-mannered middle-aged woman whom I never take to. (She says to me, "We are climbing a mountain together, you and I. I am holding the rope for you, Cole. I am here, holding the rope while you are climbing the mountain. I've got you. I'm not going to let go of this rope." She makes two fists, one on top of the other, as if grasping an imaginary rope. I think, *That thing don't look too sturdy, lady.*) We begin each weekly appointment by going over my diary card, a DBT staple. The diary card has the days of the week listed down one side followed by boxes to check. On the top are lists of emotions (sadness, shame, anger, fear, joy) and of actions or idealizations (suicide, pain, lying, drug use) and the instruction to rate one's experiences from 1 to 5 each day in the appropriate box, including a box to rate my urge to quit therapy. I want to believe that recording, rating, and reporting my emotions and urges is a step toward mastery of these emotions, and sometimes I do. Mainly, the card gives my therapist raw data on my otherwise intangible internal experiences. This raw data is then used in part to determine whether therapy is working. Not unaware of the charted weight of each number in a box, I deliberate gravely over the difference between a 4 or a 5. Anger and suicidal ideation usually get a five, along with the desire to quit therapy. I want to telegraph as much urgency as possible. I want to prove to her that my anger, sadness, and pain are so epic as to only be properly graphed seismically.

The dialectic, in short, is the concept that two opposites can both be equally true, rather than canceling each other out. The dialectic is what I hold on to in DBT; it is the concept that keeps me receptive to the program because it is what I need to hear and what I need to believe in. By my own logic, if I can start to wrap my head around the concept that I am healed and I am broken, that there is room in me to be both, then maybe I don't have to give up being broken in order to be healed.

Group is in the evenings, at seven. It always begins with meditation and then check-in, where we go around the table and talk about whom we interacted with over the past week, and it always ends with checkout. We learn a new skill, documented on a worksheet, take a break, talk about an activity in the world that we're all assigned to practice that week that involves last week's skill. (For example, if the skill is asking for things, you go into a store and ask for change or ask someone the time. I remember this assignment especially because a few people in the group reported that this particular assignment was ridiculously easy; I found it hard and kept quiet when no one else admitted to it.) We note how successful we were in completing the task and how it made us feel.

My individual therapist told me that I'm a little old for the young adult therapy group, but I find a pretty wide range of ages. There's a high school–aged boy who wants to become a weatherman. When we go around the room for check-in at the beginning of every session, each one of us talking about the past week, he always includes a report. "This week we were supposed to have showers, but the clouds didn't ever break, they just hung over us."

There's a waiter in his early twenties with big dark eyes and a scraggly beard, who often fidgets with a safety pin he's stuck through his jeans. "I pin this here on purpose. It's a coping mechanism."

The group member whom I admire and want to befriend is a young woman in law school with tattoos all over her body. The first day of group she wears short sleeves, even though it's the beginning of winter, and you can see the cuts all up and down her arms. She wears cardigans every day after that. "The group leader told me that it might be triggering for people to see my scars," she tells me once, during break. The DBT rules state that we are not allowed to make friends in group. We must never see each other outside of group or exchange information. We may be cordial but never personal. This makes the ten-minute break sandwiched between the two hours of our session predictably awkward. Most of us check our cell phones; a few go outside to smoke cigarettes.

We cannot talk about triggering in group. If we have what is called *target behavior* during the week, we can only say, "I had some target behavior this week. I called my individual therapist." Otherwise, naming your target behavior risks triggering someone else's target behavior. It also prevents us from bonding over shared behaviors, which could spin into encouraging each other in those behaviors.

Everyone in DBT has a target behavior. There are the more obvious ones: addictions, eating disorders, and self-mutilation. Then there are the less easily quantifiable, the borderline personality characteristics that the program was designed to treat.

My target behavior is freaking out. Freaking out consists of slapping myself in the face over and over. I'm pummeling my most wild self into submission. It is an urgency fueling a singular focus: destroy. Destroy self, destroy lamp, vase, turn the house over like a burglar, as if comfort is a physical object stored in a lockbox hidden behind a painting, next to my grandmother's wedding ring. I must turn everything over to find it.

I am trying desperately, with all of my force, to rip a physical rupture in the fabric of reality that I can slip inside of and disappear. In DBT language, this is referred to as *crisis behavior.*

I am taught by one of the counselors to put an ice cube on the back of my neck when I am having a panic attack. Studies of people saved from drowning in freezing water show that the heart rate and pulse are slowed by cold temperatures, she says. The freezing water that is killing them slowly is also what keeps them from dying of shock. You can get the same reaction from your body by holding a piece of ice to the back of your neck. I try it one night when I can't breathe, forcing myself to keep holding the ice to the back of my neck even though it's already freezing in the house on Belmont Street because we can't afford the heat. The water trickles down inside the neck of the heavy raincoat I've taken to wearing inside. Eventually it works — the ice water trickles down my back, dampening the neck of my sweater, and I can breathe again.

When I first entered DBT, it had never once occurred to me that I could navigate my own emotions. *Self-soothing,* as it's called in DBT, was foreign to me. We were given a Xerox with a list of "skills," actions to practice when we're feeling emotionally overwhelmed: take a hot bath, go for a walk, listen to happy music — strategies that are obvious to most people. I don't know if the reason that I did not already have this programming is neurological. I don't remember if it was a neurologist or a therapist who years later told me, "You have to stop compartmentalizing; your brain affects everything about who you are." It could have been either of them.

DBT is based on Eastern philosophy; there are worksheets with mottos and goals and drawings of lotus blossoms. Something about the roots and the muck and the beautiful flower, but it just makes me think about lotus eating and that makes me think of drugs. Engaging in drinking or drug use is another behavior that we're all supposed to avoid because it often triggers target behavior. There is a separate DBT group to treat addiction but the lines of who belongs in what group often blur in our young adult group. I switch counselors from the woman who tells me that we are climbing a mountain together and I stay in the program for so long that everyone in my original group graduates before me. The new group is all female; the one who talks the most wears scrubs with teddy bears on them to every meeting but never mentions anything about being in the medical industry. Eventually, my insurance runs out, and my period in DBT ends abruptly with a phone call from my counselor telling me that she can't see me until I get my finances figured out. We both know that there is no figuring out to do.

It wasn't so much that I decided to live as I decided not to die; setting up house in a sort of vaguely suicidal purgatory. I hadn't forgotten being hooked up to the biofeedback machine my final year of college, the rabbit ears. I don't know what people trained in biofeedback are called or how to find them; the woman who first hooked me up to the machine was trained as a naturopath, but for all I know that's a coincidence. I do an online search for "Biofeedback, Portland, OR" and email the first person to offer a free consultation, Nell, who happens to specialize in a type of biofeedback more specific to the brain called *neurofeedback*.

The afternoon after my first consultation with Nell, I walk across Northwest Twenty-third Avenue to the bar inside a trendy Thai fusion restaurant. I order a martini and pull the paperwork she had handed me out of its manila envelope. As I wait for my mom to pick me up in the family minivan, I fill out Nell's intake form.

Reason for seeking neurofeedback:
Without hesitation, I write: *I am out of options.*

I don't fully understand neurofeedback, although Nell has explained it several times. I understand that pills treat the chemical aspect of the brain, while neurofeedback treats the electrical aspect. Your brain runs on electricity. You can treat the chemical aspect of depression, but if the brain's electricity is out of whack, the pills can do only so much. We have to teach my brain to stay at a certain wavelength, a healthy one. Her computer system will train my brain to stay at a healthy wavelength, like Pavlov's dogs. What really sells me is that Nell practices neurofeedback because she walked into someone else's office thinking it was her last stop and it saved her life. Also, she's willing to work out a plan with me to pay her in installments. Sitting in Nell's office for my first consultation, I feel safe for the first time in a very long time. She says a curse word, *bullshit,* which makes me like her.

It can take anywhere from a matter of days to weeks to see results in neurofeedback, as reactions to the treatment are as varied as people's brains. For one year, twice a week, I remember to wear my hair in a ponytail. I take the bus from the essential oil factory where I'm still working when we first meet to Nell's office in the trendy shopping district. I sit in a black leather lounge chair while Nell attaches electrodes to my head. The placement of the electrodes corresponds with where the trouble is in the brain.

She hands me a clipboard, and I rate my depression and anxiety, circle numbers. I try to clear my head and stare at the screen, to relax. I tell myself that all I have to do is sit. There is a spaceship motoring through a tunnel with clouds of smoke trailing behind it on the screen before me. My brain is making the spaceship go; I can "try" to make it go, but it doesn't matter — the electricity in my brain will make it go no matter what I do. When my brain is tired, the spaceship stalls. As my brain waves become more used to being exercised, the spaceship goes more steadily.

Nell and I become friends; I trust her with my brain, which is to trust her with my life. As I sit in her chair with electrodes glued to my head, we chat about naturopathic remedies and what she feeds her cat and the continuing reign of terror brought on by her roommate's small dog. Eventually, my brain begins to go quiet. I start to scale back from seeing her twice a week.

I've already been seeing Nell for several months when I find out about the hole in my brain. She recommends Dr. Z, a neurological chiropractor. I resist. I am broke, only able to see Nell because she allows me to pay when I can, and what the hell is a neurological chiropractor anyway? I can take only so much alternative healing. "I can't afford him," I tell her dismissively. Anyway, I'm leaving for grad school in September, so we would only have the rest of the summer to work together.

The first time that I applied for MFA writing programs, in a halfhearted attempt to grab hold of some idea of a future to get me through my depression, I couldn't keep track of all of the forms, and all of my applications were either late or incomplete. This year, just getting the applications in on time felt like a major victory. Getting into California Institute of the Arts means that I get to feel good at something again for the first time since I graduated from college, three years ago, and I am desperate to feel good at something again. My gut instinct is that in order to do that I have to leave the "broken" parts of myself here in Portland; as if I could pick and choose what parts of my brain get to go to grad school.

I am trying to appear firm in my arguments, which is difficult to pull off with my skull covered in electrodes. The gooey paste that attaches them to my skin is sliding down my forehead. "Well, he'd probably treat you for free because he'll want to write a case study on you for a medical journal." I imagine myself on the cover of *Neurological Chiropractor's Weekly.* I relent and call his office, leaving a cryptic message with his secretary about being a special case recommended by Nell. He calls me the next morning. He talks like a surfer: "Come into the office. We'll figure out this whole strange trip you're on." As when I started seeing

Nell, I tell myself that I don't have much to lose.

■ ■ ■ ■

III.

PERSEVERANCE

■ ■ ■ ■

"Would you tell me, please, which way I
    ought to go from here?"
"That depends a good deal on where you
    want to get to," said the Cat.
"I don't much care where —" said Alice.
"Then it doesn't matter which way you go,"
    said the Cat.
"— so long as I get SOMEWHERE," Alice
    added as an explanation.
"Oh, you're sure to do that," said the Cat,
    "if you only walk long enough."
            — Lewis Carroll, *Alice in Wonderland*

June 2007
Portland, Oregon

During the summer of my diagnosis, I'm living in Northeast Portland with a hip twentysomething couple in a key lime–colored house. John builds custom amps for a living and hangs out with rock stars. Astrid is a beautiful Swedish woman who trains horses. They seem incredibly nice and deeply in love. I have a room downstairs, and they live upstairs. I try not to let the cats out. Sometimes we all have beers in the living room and watch their latest Netflix order. More often, I just duck my head out of my room now and again and try not to get too much of their bliss on me. I think of myself as the mildly eccentric but nice-enough female boarder, like a peripheral character in a Dickens novel.

A week or so after that afternoon in Dr. Volt's office, I come home from work and pass John, bent over his laptop on the living room couch. "How are you?" he asks. What is amazing about John is not only that he asks this, but also that often, he genuinely wants to know. "I've got a hole in my brain," I say, shrugging. I had said some vague things to Astrid about seeing the neurologist, so this information isn't coming completely out of left field, but now I'm trying to play off my shock as indifference.

"Dude, that's nothing. I knew a guy in high school who had a hole in his penis . . . I mean, in *the side.*"

I stare at him, which apparently encourages further explanation. "He used to . . . *streeetch* it out during homeroom." John mimics stretching with his hands.

"Wow. That's, um, crazy," I say.

"Yeah." John nods.

I want a cure, a cast, a shot, a surgery. Isn't that how this works? The doctor finds a break and heals it. The neuropsychologist whom Dr. Volt refers me to looks like a midwestern housewife or a kindergarten teacher, generically maternal. I imagine that her demeanor left her no choice. She was drafted into a life of nurturing the disabled and soon began donning the costumes required of her role: denim dresses with sunflower appliqués. Today's ensemble is a beige tunic and a long strand of turquoise glass beads. I am eager to begin my rehabilitation.

I approach the neuropsychologist as if she were my physical therapist. Together, we will strengthen my brain as if it were a muscle instead of a vital organ. It's a natural concept: I am sick, I will get better. I am weak, I will become strong. Now that we've identified the problem, we can begin working toward the solution.

If Dr. Volt had said that there was nothing to be done, I would like to believe that I would have worked toward accepting that. But no one has ever said that because no one can really say. What we know about the brain will always be outweighed by what we don't know about it. This is as much an advantage as it is a disadvantage.

"What are we going to do together?" I ask. "There must be something akin to physical therapy for this, like they have for stroke victims."

She furrows her brow. "There is no physical therapy. Our time together is more about compensating than strengthening."

I don't know what to make of this; surely there must be more we can do. Put me on a treadmill, strap electrodes to my head, bring out the flash cards — I'm begging you. I'm an eager student, ready to practice skill sets and strategies.

She pauses for a moment. "Have you ever considered a guide dog?"

She asks me to complete a test involving drawing dots on lines with a No. 2 pencil. While I draw dots on the lines, I fantasize about the dog.

The second and last time we meet, the neuropsychologist, who cannot prescribe medication, suggests a prescription for Wellbutrin and slides a photocopied chapter from *Driven to Distraction* across her desk to me. (My mother has owned a copy of this classic ADD/ADHD tome since my ADD phase in the early 1990s.) This is it? A prescription for antidepressants and a photocopied chapter from a book on ADD are my "tools for coping"?

I show her a printout of the MRI; she stares at the photo and then at me, saying nothing. No one had given the neuropsychologist my MRI results. This is like the first faux pas on a blind date. Starting with the first signs of abnormality during my testing with Dr. Volt and his resident, and continuing to my quickly scheduled battery of tests and X-rays and, then, all the time that Dr. Volt dedicated to helping me and my family understand my "condition," I had been wooed by the medical establishment. I have the email addresses and phone numbers of everyone who's treated me; I've been encouraged to stay in touch. There is that moment when you can look back at a failed romantic relationship and spot the first sign of trouble. Excuses that sounded valid at the time seem so obviously preposterous when viewed through the lens of the aftermath. I look back at this moment, when I debriefed my new neuropsychologist on my condition and we huddled together over a printout of the email attachment that contained my MRI, and think now that this was where it all began. I should have known that the medical industry and I were at best a bittersweet match. I don't want coping strategies; I want strengthening exercises. I want a plan, goals, strategies, charted progress. I want to get better.

"This is Chris Smith, calling from Dr. Volt's office. I have the number for a guide dog for you." The number he gives me is for Guide Dogs for the Blind. "Call them up — we should be able to get the ball rolling on this guide-dog situation. And here's my number — please give me a call if you run into any speed bumps."

"I will — thank you so much for getting in touch with me!"

And then he ends with the words I've been waiting so long to hear: "I will be an advocate for your disability needs."

I call the local number Chris Smith left me, and a woman connects me to the California office to start my intake.

"Guide Dogs for the Blind," the woman on the line says flatly.

"Hi. I'm inquiring about a guide dog. I'm not sure where to begin. I was referred by my neurologist; I'm fully sighted, but I have a neurological . . . condition. I have a difficult time judging how far and fast objects are moving in space. It's a sort of spatial blindness, I guess."

"So, I'm sorry — you are fully sighted?"

"Yes. I was hoping that a dog would help me with crossing the street or getting through a crowd, since I have a difficult time with moving objects."

"Well. That's not exactly how it works. First of all, you have to be legally blind to receive a dog from us. Second of all, even if we could give you a dog, it wouldn't do what you want it to. That's not how it works. The guide dog doesn't tell a blind person when to cross the street. The *handler* listens to traffic, makes a judgment, and then gives the sign when to cross."

"Oh. I see."

"So I'm afraid we can't help you with a dog."

"I see."

"But how about a cane?" she says.

"A cane?"

"Yes, you know, a cane."

"But — OK — correct me if I'm wrong here. How exactly does a cane work?"

"Well, it would detect an object on the street. Like litter, or the curb, or a person."

"But I am fully sighted."

"Right."

I try a new tack.

"So . . . OK. It sounds like a cane is for trouble with immobile objects."

"Yes."

"And I have problems with mobile objects."

"Right."

"So, I'm not sure how a cane would help me."

"That's true. That's a good point."

We are both momentarily silent.

"Well, a cane would notify drivers of your disability. Drivers would see the cane and slow down. You should really look into a cane. Well, anyway, they wouldn't be able to give you a cane unless you went through training. You meet with a person about how to get around town more easily. But that would be the Oregon Commission for the Blind. Here, let me give you their number."

"But . . . I'm not blind."

"Yes, I understand. But in order to get a cane you need to go through training, and the training might be helpful for you. It's meeting with a person who shows you how to navigate about town."

If I want help, I need to fit under a code so that people and companies and governments can receive funds in exchange for helping me. There is no template for how to help me, but there is a template for aiding the blind. If I can slide into someone else's code, it may be my only bet for receiving any services. So I take the number and thank this woman and hang up, in part because I lack the energy to explain to her that first, I would have to teach my teacher how I get around town based on visual landmarks. I am going to the blind to learn how to see. I think Simon and Garfunkel wrote a song about this once.

I wish that if people couldn't help me, they would just say, "I'm terribly sorry, I can't help you." Sometimes it's really hard for both the other party and me to tell where this line is. It's a line that no one wants to cross unless they are certain.

I call Chris Smith's office.

"Hi, I've run into a road bump. I called the number you gave me, and I spoke to a woman in intake. She offered me a cane, which is . . . not exactly what I'm in the market for."

"Right. Because you're talking about spatial motility issues. A cane wouldn't help you."

"Right."

Waves of relief run off me that are so strong I swear I can see them — little black squiggly lines of steam.

"Well, I'll call them back and explain. We may have to get Dr. Volt involved, and he may have to call them as well. But we'll get this all sorted out, don't worry."

"Oh, thank you so much! Can I just ask you one question?"

"Of course."

"What is your position at Dr. Volt's office?"

"I'm a licensed clinical social worker. I usually teach new doctors how to work with social services, but Dr. Volt asked me to look into your file."

"*A social worker!* That's, that's so great! Thank you!"

"No problem."

And then he says it *again:* "Don't worry, Dr. Volt and I are here to advocate for your disability."

I don't call the Oregon Commission for the Blind. A week later, I am writing in a coffee shop when I get a call from Chris Smith; I walk outside to take it.

"Well, it seems that Dr. Volt and I have run into a few stumbling blocks as well."

"Oh, really?"

"It seems that in order to get you the training to get around, you'd have to be legally blind."

This being the Oregon Commission for the Blind we're talking about, I can't say I'm shocked.

"Dr. Volt is going to write a note explaining your situation. You must be really frustrated."

The conversation with the guide-dog lady exhausted me.

I hear him say, "You must feel al—" Then he changes his tactic: "Do you feel all alone in this process?"

I am deeply thankful to be able to participate at all in the medical system. It is, however, a *system* first. I am an anomaly, which is a pretty valid reason for feeling alone in this process. I want to say: my job, your job, is to fit me into a system that relies inherently on templates so that I may receive care or aid. If you had any idea how much I depend on you, a voice on the phone, a complete stranger, to enhance my daily quality of life and how helpless that makes me feel, you would not ask me a question like that. You ask me a question like that, and I cry and you comfort me, and I thank you and you get to hang up feeling as if you've done something, but I hang up without services. I am not going to break down, and you are not going to comfort me.

I am holding back tears as I say to him, dryly, "No, I am just very frustrated, and I'm sure that you and Dr. Volt are as well." I am thankful that my voice does not quaver as he promises to be in touch, and I thank him and hang up. We never speak again.

"Yowza!" Dr. Z, the neurological chiropractor Nell referred me to, turns away from his laptop as if it just bit him. When I peer over his screen, I can see the digital scan of my MRI. "Did you see my neck snap back like that?" he asks me. I smile timidly, not sure if I'm supposed to be proud or embarrassed, feeling both.

He slides on his stool in a sleek swooping motion in my direction like a steel-limbed satyr, born part stool, and leans toward me as if to confide a secret.

"Do you shave your legs?" he asks.

"Yes." I nod my head vigorously.

"Do you cut yourself often?"

"No, not really. But sometimes I forget to . . . shave one leg."

Dr. Z's eyebrows shoot up. It's that look that I'm learning to recognize; a medical discovery is taking place.

"Which leg?"

"I . . . don't know."

"The left one," he counters with certainty. I shrug and laugh. "OK, the left one."

He slides backward on the stool, without looking behind him, and abruptly brakes to a dead stop. "The hydrocephalus, the water in your brain, is on the right side. The right side of the brain controls the left side of the body. We know you've got some left/right confusion going on. I'm willing to bet you've got some hemineglect happening."

"Hemineglect," I parrot.

"You don't recognize things on your left side. You *see* them, but your brain ignores them, or it takes longer for your brain to process them. You favor things, people, on your right side."

"OK," I say, lamely. I am right-handed; that's about all that I can vouch for.

"Stand up. We're going to do an experiment."

I jump off of the examining table, and Dr. Z stands up and approaches me. He is standing in front of me, a few inches away.

"OK," he says, stepping to my side. "What side am I on now?"

I twitch my fingers on the side of my body that he's standing closest to and mime writing my name.

"Right?"

"Yes, right. OK, how ya feeling?"

"OK."

"So."

He takes one long, swaggering step to the other side of my body. My stomach flip-flops.

"And now?"

"Oh, yeah. Don't do that," I snap reflexively.

Surprised by my own reaction, I smile apologetically. He laughs.

"See?"

I nod.

"This makes you uncomfortable."

I nod again, slowly. I'm becoming increasingly annoyed with this new game, which only makes Dr. Z more gleeful.

"Yeah, this maybe makes you anxious?"

I look down at the floor.

"My stomach feels queasy."

"Exactly!" Dr. Z nods enthusiastically. "Sooooo . . ." He swoops back over to my right, and I ease up instantly. "We have to exercise that left side of yours."

When I apply this information retroactively to reframe my day-to-day life, it fits so well into my experience that I'm surprised that I've never considered it. I often feel crowded or anxious, and because of that I have tended to think of myself as difficult or antisocial. Since I am not conscious of which is my left or right side, it never occurred to me until now that I'm more often uncomfortable when approached from the left, especially by strangers. I always considered my sensation of queasiness a symptom of my anxiety; I figured that my stomach was flip-flopping because I was nervous, not knowing until now that my disorientation is rooted in a physical condition. Until Dr. Z's experiment I never realized how much the churning in my stomach feels like motion sickness.

I now know that the queasy feeling in my stomach when a vehicle whizzes toward me or past me at an incalculable speed should not be dismissed. Its origins are rooted in both a physical manifestation of my weakened perception and the reality that a car is headed in my direction at an incalculable speed, which also induces anxiety.

Each time I sit in Dr. Z's waiting room for weekly sessions that summer before leaving for grad school, I bring the same book, an oral history of the postpunk movement. He tells me that my craving for repetitive four-chord structure is linked to the weakness in my right parietal. I need to strengthen my brain, not coddle it. This means moving all of the folders on my computer to my left side, sitting to the right of the professor in my grad school workshops, anything to force my right brain to process information coming from my left side. He prescribes highly structured classical music and opera in foreign languages, preferably non-Germanic because it is less like English, to be listened to through the left headphone only. I try, but it is like tightening my head in a vise; it makes every muscle in my body tighten in resistance, which must be the point.

"Do you remember learning to tie your shoes?" my mother asks.

"No, I know it was late. How old was I?"

"I don't know, I just remember that we kept having to buy you Velcro shoes because

131

you couldn't get the hang of tying them."

I laugh. In my memory, I had Velcro shoes because I *liked* Velcro shoes, but I realize that she's right. I liked them not just for the sound of the Velcro ripping but because they fastened without laces. Tying one's shoes really is a complex process, if you stop to think about it — all of the places that your fingers have to go, when to release the knot, when to loop; it's a deft bit of handiwork.

"We kept showing you, kept teaching you little tricks, but it wouldn't stick."

"Well, eventually I got the hang of it," I say.

"Yes, you know how to tie your shoes now. Right? Do you know how to tie your shoes now?" my mother asks.

"Yes, Mom, I know how to tie my shoes." Then, while I'm on the phone with her, I examine my shoe collection. Pink ballet flats, black zip-up boots with wooden heels, dark red wedges, slip-on sneakers. "Oh my God, I don't even own any shoes with laces." I rack my brain and remember a pair of rubber-soled boots with laces that I left at home in Portland because they were too warm to bring to California. OK, one pair. Good.

"You need to go to a shoe store to make sure that you can still tie shoes," Mom says.

"Mom, obviously I know how to tie my shoes. I just . . . it would seem that I still prefer not to."

"And then there's the grocery store. The vegetables are always to the left or right, and the dairy is always in the back because everyone needs milk and they want to make you walk through the whole store."

I pause. "This is a mystifying conversation," I say.

She sighs. "I know, I know, but how many grocery stores have you been in in your life?"

"Well, that's sort of the point, isn't it?"

"We've never really talked about this before, have we?" she asks.

"This is what I worry about," she says, and I feel rotten. "I've seen you; I know you have this much trouble in a grocery store. But then let's go to the next step: there's a box store. And then bigger than that: there's the mall. And then after that there's downtown, there's figuring out the bus and the streets and where to get off and once you're off how to figure out which way you're headed, and then, after all that, let's say you have a job interview."

"I know."

She's referring to my recent search for a job in Portland before I learned I had been accepted to grad school. I was late to or completely missed several interviews, and when I did show up I was a wreck, sweaty and anxious, already worried about the trip home. Eventually, my parents began picking me up and dropping me off for job interviews. I am unemployed and being chauffeured around by my parents. I have begun to wonder why I went to college at all. My mother continues, "And then there's bigger cities . . ."

"And backpacking through Europe," I say.

This sounds snide, which is not what I meant, so I try to explain: "Joe just got back from Europe; people backpack through Europe by themselves. This is, like, a thing that people do. They do it in books all the time. I've always wanted to do that."

My mom says, "I just think . . . even if you went with someone, you'd just be so confused and dragged around by people that I don't think you'd even enjoy it."

When I was a child and my father still had the job in public relations, we traded houses with families in other countries several times. We put up a listing for our house, in Berwyn, a suburb of Philadelphia, with a description that included the number of our bedrooms and bathrooms and cars and pets, and if someone from Paris or Barcelona who was also listed in the book of listings wanted to swap houses with us for a month, they would send us a letter. That was how we went to Europe. I was a child then and not expected to do anything other than tag along. Now, as an adult, I am dead weight.

If I'm going on a road trip, I print out the directions from a map site in list form, so that I can read them to the driver instead of looking at a map. To my credit, I am also an excellent playlist maker and snack provider. And I never ask if we are there yet.

"Do you remember," I ask my mother, "did I seem this afraid of crossing the street before? It's getting so I'm getting confused and I can't remember straight."

"Well, if other kids wanted candy, they would just run across the street to the candy store," she says. "But you always wanted to wait, to go with someone else. And when we crossed streets, you always stayed close. I didn't think anything of it; I figured if you wanted to wait to cross the street with me, well, that was fine. But you were the first. Maybe if I had Carly or Marni to compare you to, and they were crossing streets on their own and you weren't, maybe then I would have been worried. And then when you got older, you learned to hide it; you just crossed when all your friends crossed, and you learned to hide it from yourself as well."

"All that happens is that you're more cautious than other people when you cross the street," one of my friends later weighs in, and I nod. But I'm thinking, *That's all that happens to you.* I pause, I frown, I hesitate, I pause again, I wait, maybe put a foot out, and eventually I cross. I'm striking a terrifying bargain between the moving object (a car), and a fixed object (myself). I can't really say what I thought of this before the diagnosis because I didn't know that there was anything to think about it. When I did get down on myself for being so cautious, it fell under the umbrella of being a generally anxious person. It hadn't occurred to me that I might be anxious because I was processing information differently from the way other people process it; I didn't think about processing information at all. The generally anxious person crosses the street to get to the other side, just as the person with the neurological condition or the blind person does. Like the crossing chicken, I thought "why" was beside the point. At the time, thinking about crossing seemed to be the problem itself, rather than a step toward a solution.

Dr. Volt wants my father to have an MRI too. Everyone — Volt, my father, my mother, my sisters, me — is certain my father will have a black hole like mine on his MRI. It's the only explanation as to why my father and I are both terrible at math, horrible with directions, and unable to keep track of time. We are not allowed to partner off on errands together, lest my mother or my sister Carly be sent in to retrieve us when we become lost or forget why we even set out on the road to begin with.

My mom and I are seated across from each other in a wooden booth in a coffee shop down the street from Nell's office. Mom has just picked me up from my latest neurofeedback appointment with Nell, and now we're waiting together for my father to call from Dr. Volt's office with the results of his MRI. If he has a hole in his brain as well, it may prove that a genetic link is the cause of the atrophy. However, these holes with cranial fluid in the brain are more common than most people realize, though not usually as large as mine. If my father also has a hole in his brain, the next step will be to call in my sisters for scans. Dr. Volt has urged us to get in touch with relatives on my father's side who may be willing to have an MRI, but most of my father's side of the family are Orthodox Jews who don't speak to us.

One of my fondest memories of hanging out with my father is when he picked me up from my job selling books at the Borders in the newly opened Bridgeport Village, a ritzy mall in the suburbs. It's the only open-air mall in Portland, where it rains nine months out of the year, but a little rain never got in the way of anyone's lust for Egyptian linen or sea-salt scrubs.

That day, my father stepped out of his car, surveyed the landscape of lunching ladies and manicured teenagers with armfuls of shopping bags, and proclaimed in his thick New York accent, "All of these people deserve to have hot molten lava poured down their throats." I loved him for saying loudly and succinctly what all of us working there spent all day thinking to ourselves.

It was not as much fun, however, when I brought home my first boyfriend and my father looked him over and quickly labeled him "mediocre." Or when he tells me that I don't really need that bowl of ice cream. The man has no filter and no interest in attaining one. He also has three daughters and one wife, who volley back, or cry, or yell, or sulk, or stomp away to their respective rooms. While our reactions vary, his do not. "Can't you take a joke?" he says. Sometimes we can, sometimes we can't. Humor is our best defense, to deflect the joke back at him or draw attention to another relative. When I'm the target, I'll shoot back a joke about Marni's nipple rings getting stuck in her sweater. This is how we show love, and how we survive.

I anxiously play with the straw in my iced coffee. My mom is gripping her cell phone. "If he doesn't . . . if it comes up clean, well, then, I guess I just married an asshole."

The phone rings. There is a short burst of chatter, ending with my mother asking my father, "Well, what now?" She snaps the phone shut. "No hole. Clean." She is clearly disappointed. Shock is becoming a familiar sensation rooted in my stomach. It's official. I am the only one with this condition. I hadn't realized how much I had been counting on my father's company, partially resenting sharing this with him and also grateful for a physical validation of our link.

When my father is overtaken by dark periods of depression, he always turns to me and intones, "You know how it is." He has witnessed my own dark periods. When complicated theories come easily to me, I know it is his gift that I am using. I was certain that we shared this too — that the vague sense that he and I were more strongly linked, for better or for worse, than he and my other sisters, would be brought to light on the stark, undeniable film of an MRI.

When we get home, my dad tells me that Dr. Volt asked him if he had any difficulties telling time. "I explained to him that time is merely a construct. That's Hegel," he says, gleefully.

Ever since I can remember, when either of my sisters or I have complained about doing the dishes or other chores, my father will intone, "Aristotle says, 'There is no justice in the family.' " I probably wasn't even ten yet when my father first asked me whether a tree falling in a forest makes a sound if no one is around to witness it. I am still learning how to answer him.

(Months later, while I am studying writing at CalArts, my mother begins reading about a condition called Asperger's Syndrome. She begs my father to call Dr. Volt and set up a screening. My father calls the receptionist, who puts him straight on the phone with Dr. Volt. After an hour-long conversation with my father, he says, "Don't

140

bother coming in for a formal screening. You've got it.")

"Do you remember my parents?" my mom asks. I am sitting with her at my parents' kitchen table. Taken off guard by this new line of questioning, I'm unsure of how to proceed.

"Yeah . . . of course I remember."

"What do you remember?"

I squirm and shrug and try to answer her question. "They were always very nice to me; I don't know, I was really young when they died."

"You were twelve."

"Oh. I guess that's not that young."

Silence.

"Your mom liked musicals. Grandpa bought me a dollhouse once, and it made me kind of anxious because it cost like a hundred dollars, which to me at the time was like a huge fortune — why are you asking me this now?"

"Amy said I should. She says I have no identity of my own."

I furrow my brow. Amy is my mom's therapist. She is in her early or midthirties; I remember that her office is decorated with photographs of distant and exotic lands she's visited with her husband. I went to her a couple of times, but we never really clicked the way that she has with my mom, who loves her. Not long after I stopped seeing her, she suggested to Mom that I attend Dialectical Behavior Therapy.

"You're a really good mother," I say.

"Yeah. Amy says I have no identity outside of being a mother."

I don't know how to begin to answer this.

She suggests more appointments with specialists, more exercises and strategies. If I am cured, who does my mother become?

July 2007
Seattle, Washington

I'm meeting Minerva at her brother Charlie's place in Seattle to work out plans for her wedding next summer. Minerva and I have only recently been back in touch — she found me online earlier this summer — but we've quickly picked up where we left off in high school. A friend who worked with me at the essential oil factory is driving to Seattle from Portland, and she agrees to drop me off at Charlie's apartment.

I arrive in the early evening. Charlie opens the door, shakes my hand firmly and brusquely, and then sits down at his desk. He looks back up at me standing in the middle of his apartment and just stares at me, expressionless. I remember his intense green eyes from when we first met in the art room ten years ago. In that moment I make a secret decision about Charlie that I won't tell myself until winter. I store it away like a squirrel until it gets cold out and I need more to survive on.

Minerva walks in from the kitchen and gives me a big hug. "Hi! How *are* you?"

She seems like a different person from the loud, opinionated, irresistible girl that I hung out with in the art room at lunch hour. Minerva is finishing up a degree at Georgetown law; her new fiancé is also a lawyer. How do people do this? Commit to a track, a person, and a career? I have no idea. Her certainty frightens me. I've been to only a couple of weddings of friends my age, both of which left me feeling as if I'd just watched a school play. I wanted to encourage and congratulate the newlyweds, but I also felt awkward. I am hoping that participating in Minerva's wedding might change my feelings somehow.

"There won't be any bridesmaids, but I'd like you to be my official wedding buddy." She and I sit on the couch and chat about the dress that her mother is making her while Charlie bounds around the room, ignoring us completely. He picks up a tangle of cords from his desk, screws open the back of an old Casio keyboard, and puts it down in favor of another old keyboard, begins ripping some knobs off it, goes outside to check out his tomato plants in the front window of the apartment, steps back inside.

When he steps back in, Minerva and I are sitting over my laptop, looking at the site for a label that specializes in re-creating dress patterns from the 1940s. I point out a navy blue dress with an iris embroidered on the shoulder. "That's the one I'm thinking about wearing, if I can afford it."

"I think my wedding dress is going to be knee length," Minerva says. While we've been talking, I haven't been able to stop tracking Charlie's jerking movements as he busies himself around the apartment. When he steps outside again, I whisper, "What's up with Charlie?"

"Oh, his back hurts. It hurts for him to sit still. His back hurts most of the time; walking around helps." She shrugs, but she doesn't meet my eyes as she explains, "Scoliosis. His spine is basically a question mark. The nurse caught it at school; you know those checks everyone has to do, touch your toes? I have it a little bit too but not nearly as much. Anyway, our parents *weren't* exactly *together* enough to do anything about it." Minerva often emphasizes every other word when she speaks; Charlie almost never stresses words.

We step outside and find him downstairs

in the parking lot, adjusting the handlebars on his motorcycle, a black machine with a body like a wasp. "It's a redesign of a Kawasaki from the seventies," he begins, gesturing up and down the handlebars and around the body of the machine as he talks about each piece. While neither Minerva nor I care about the mechanics of Charlie's motorcycle, we can't bring ourselves to interrupt him. There's a soft-spoken persuasiveness in his tone, a level of investment in the people who are listening to him that I didn't expect from a man intent on explaining how something mechanical works to two women standing in a parking lot.

The next morning, we stop at a nearby coffee shop and take our coffees to Green Lake, the park next to Charlie's apartment building. Minerva and I are in the empty playground sitting on one of those merry-go-round-type structures, the ones that you ride by kicking off the ground with your feet until there's a strong spin going, and then you place both feet on the metal floor as it goes faster and faster and you get dizzy, and once it slows down you do it again. Charlie is pushing it for us as he explains to us how subprime lending works. He just helped his mother sell her house in Sacramento, the house that they grew up in, moving her into an apartment. I am less than half listening to him. His drone is lost in the wind as Minerva and I spin.

"Faster, Charlie, faster!" Minerva yells, and Charlie rolls his jacket sleeves up and gives us a big push. He hops up on the nearby picnic table between spins.

When we get back to Charlie's apartment, Minerva says casually, "You want to see some pictures?"

She pulls out a stack of photographs. The photos are of piles of garbage, rolls of paper towels, bags of McDonald's, empty soda cans, plastic liter soda jugs. "It's my mom's house, before we cleaned it up and sold it."

I had been to their mom's house once or twice during my high school years. I remember high ceilings and a constant hum of anxiety, as if the whole house was an ornament hanging from a string. I don't know how it is I don't remember the mess, but it must have been there then. It must have been the origin of the incessant twinge of tension that Minerva seems, at least externally, dulled to.

I look away from the pictures, embarrassed. "That's about what I expected," I say quietly. It's not, though. Minerva and Charlie were like Hansel and Gretel, two children in a dark fairy tale. I thought that I knew what their world was like because I'd heard their stories, but I didn't have a clue.

September 2007
Valencia, California

In the bag I receive during CalArts orientation is a keychain with the logo of the city of Santa Clarita, the town next door, SANTA CLARITA — 1987, the year when the town was incorporated. I was six. Valencia, a suburb about an hour and forty-five minutes away from Los Angeles, is best known for its Six Flags amusement park. It is also home to a Walmart, a Target, and strings of gated suburban houses with names like Artist's Terrace.

My old Portland roommate and college friend Miranda volunteers to fly with me from Portland, sparing me the otherwise inevitable caravan with my parents. She is finishing up a degree in naturopathic medicine. My dad calls her "the Not a Doctor" and asks if she "tells people that their chi is fucked up."

149

At the Orange County Airport, we pick up the rental car, buy cheap whiskey, lemonade, and fried chicken at the grocery store, and head to the Motel 6 where we'll be spending tonight. We take a brief swim in the motel pool and then towel off and climb onto the queen-sized bed with our dinner. We wipe our greasy hands on toilet paper and yell at the *America's Top Model* marathon on TV.

In the morning, I wake up bleary-eyed and smelling of fried chicken. The sun blasts through the thin motel shades. Miranda drives to the 99 Cents Only Store, where I pick up odds and ends for my new room: hangers, detergent, a trash can, and a laundry bag.

When we arrive on campus, Miranda decides where my mirror goes best, where to place the hooks for my purses and cardigans, where my shoes go in my closet. She walks up and down the halls of CalArts' main building with two copies of the map we were given during orientation week. On the copy that I will keep with me once she leaves, she marks arrows in green highlighter marking paths to the main stairwell, the library, and the cafeteria. Her written directions, broken down into steps with noted visual landmarks, accompany the translated map.

The hardest part is envisioning how to set up systems and routines. The second-hardest part is maintaining them. I am habit Teflon. Routines do not stick.

In Valencia, the only places in walking distance of graduate housing are two strip malls containing negligible variations on the same stores. A Starbucks here, a Peet's there, this way a Vons, and that way a Safeway. I tell myself that being unable to leave Valencia of my own accord has a lot to do with one's mind-set. I am a monk; art school is my abbey.

The walls of the school are constantly repainted: one day beige, one day blue, one day pink. Every Thursday there is gallery night, where art students exhibit in the main gallery and everyone drinks wine from Trader Joe's and eats cheese and walks around and pretends that we are in an art gallery instead of a giant hall with linoleum floors that looks like a high school gym.

In the mornings, I can hear the gamelan troupe practicing from my room. When I stop for coffee in the cafeteria, there's always the same girl wearing the same leopard-print lingerie and ripped fishnets, toddling around on the same pair of broken black kitten heels. She wears a small heart-shaped sticker on her face, which sometimes moves from one cheek to the other. I quickly learn not to visit the bathroom across from the dance auditorium because the seats are splattered with vomit left behind by bulimic dance students.

On the walk back from class, every so often I see a bearded campus security officer in his dark blue uniform peel open a tin of cat food and place it on the ground for the tribe of feral cats who live in the bushes. When he comes back, the tin will be empty.

In the campus housing unit I share with an actor, a photographer, a filmmaker, and a stage manager, the locked cabinet holding the radiator and air conditioning emits a pulsing screech for possibly one minute at random hours.

I pretend to myself that I'm writing from an SRO in New York in the 1940s by wearing my maroon thrift-store kimono, pouring three-dollar-a-bottle red wine into a glass tumbler, and sitting in front of my laptop. As long as I keep the shades drawn to block the view of the main building, I can properly place myself in the role of a formerly renowned author of pulp lesbian novels, now down on her luck and forced to move into a seedy hotel. Sometimes I put on some

Nico and pretend that I am in the Chelsea Hotel instead. "Chelsea Hotel" is a much more straightforward distraction involving putting on a pair of tight jeans, ironing my hair, and smoking pot with my upstairs neighbors.

Pot boils time down to a syrup, slows a day down to molasses. It evens the playing field. In the thick haze of getting high, no one keeps track of *where* or *when,* and you've got a built-in excuse for losing track of time, homework, your keys. All that matters is what's in front of you, and if you can't find what's in front of you, you just sit back and relax until, inevitably, a new sparkly proposition or personality comes around to entertain you.

Being a little slow, a bit flaky, just disorganized, cushions all expectations, all the sharp angles of responsibility, in bubble wrap.

Being a fuckup is an excuse as flimsy as it is sturdy. It's a container for the cluttered detritus of all my smaller mistakes, like losing track of papers, books, classrooms, and time.

December 2007
Seattle, Washington

Charlie had sent me a brief email earlier in the semester telling me that I could stay at his place in Seattle if I wanted to come visit him and Minerva while I'm in Portland on winter break. Now, in December, I'm here, but Minerva is nowhere to be found. She is at her fiancé's parents' house in the suburbs. She texts me throughout the day about the flower arrangements she's going over with her fiancé's mom, and as it gets dark she decides to stay there for the night.

I'm at a bit of a loss for how to behave alone around Charlie, but he had mentioned something about a bottle of whiskey in his cupboard, and tonight I don't need to do much convincing to get him to pop out two glasses and the bottle. We sit on his couch with our glasses, drinking to alleviate the awkwardness between us. He turns to put music on, a Tom Waits album, and I can see the curved landscape of his back beneath his black T-shirt. It looks like his shoulders are crowding each other for room, an anatomical fault line where the geologic plates of his body disagree.

I show him a picture of my MRI on his laptop, as if it's a party gag. It's been seven months since it was taken, but I still feel as if the image is superimposed on my face for all to see. He shows me an X-ray of his spine, twisted into a question mark as Minerva said. I ask him if it hurts, and he says quietly, "All the time, to varying degrees."

On his laptop, he shows me a photo of a famous mathematician whose spine and limbs are so twisted up in angles that he resembles a Picasso portrait. "Charles Proteus Steinmetz. I pasted a copy of that photo on my math textbook cover in high school. Bent. I like to think of us as bent."

He tells me the story of another famous mathematician who became so enamored of the story of Snow White and the evil queen that he eventually killed himself by eating an apple he laced with poison.

"Alan Turing, the British computer scientist, was found dead by his housekeeper, a half-eaten apple next to his bed. It was the fifties. Two years earlier, Turing was given the choice of jail for acts of homosexuality or a dose of chemically castrating hormones; he chose the hormones. He was obsessed with *Snow White,* the Disney cartoon, especially the wicked witch. The apple was laced with cyanide."

We fall in love with fairy tales and mythologies; the ones we grow up with, the ones we inherit, and the ones we create for ourselves. Since my MRI, I have been turning the story of my childhood over and over in my head like a riddle. (*Why is a raven like a writing desk?*)

I'm now groping for my bearings in the same place where I have always lived: my body. Sometimes — for example, when I'm trying to navigate my way toward a destination for the first time — this new information about my neurological sense, or lack of sense, of perception clicks so sharply into focus that I feel dizzy, sick, physically overwhelmed by a fresh clarity about my own functioning. I am frightened by this new person who I have always been.

This diagnosis feels half of a gesture, a key without a lock to turn in it. My instinct is to act on this information, but how? I see different doctors or neuropsychologists, I write about it, sometimes I talk about it, trying to find the proper corresponding action to this new information about myself. I meet other people jiggling their own keys of insight into their own sets of mismatched locks, in therapy, at bars, in writing workshops. Sometimes we trade keys just to see if that will make any difference.

Charlie gestures back to the photo of the small pretzel-twisted man. "Steinmetz renamed himself at Ellis Island, when he was forced to flee Germany due to his socialist leanings. He chose his middle name, Proteus, from a nickname his German professors had given him, for the shape-shifting sea god." We're leaning together over his laptop, our knees touching, then our hands.

Being seen for the first time by someone new, feeling desirable for the first time since my diagnosis, I want to see myself as he sees me, as he sees himself. I want my pain to make me special too, like the scientists he reveres or the writers I admire.

Charles Dodgson, better known as Lewis Carroll, the author of *Alice in Wonderland,* wrote himself into his story as the Dodo because he had a stutter that forced him to pronounce his own last name "Do-do-do-Dodgson."

"I just need to move my arm," Charlie announces awkwardly, first putting it on the couch behind me and then pulling me closer to him.

We make out for a while, then he says, "I'd like you to stay in my bed tonight." He has this manner of speaking where everything sounds declarative.

I say, "OK."

He says, "And I'd like you to take your dress off."

In contrast to my aversion to touch, sex pulls me out of the world of language; it's an escape from the constant running narration in my head. Then the trouble becomes about vulnerability, rough terrain for anyone who learned early on that masking your weaknesses is the only way to avoid embarrassment. However, there are different kinds of vulnerability, and one kind can look and feel like another. Nakedness can be a way to feel seen without actually risking being known.

I laugh and say "OK" again and start to unzip my dress, which has a fire engine pattern on it, as if it was made out of old pajamas. His bed is a loft, and not long after I climb into it he has his hands tight around my neck. In the split second between that moment when I push his hands down and

158

when he moves them gently to my hips and keeps them there, I remember that we are essentially strangers and of course this interaction is all based on assumptions. But I'm desperate to be seen, and I want us both to keep making and testing assumptions for now.

The next day is New Year's Eve. I'm heading back to Portland with the friend who originally dropped me off in Seattle, who's having a party at her house. Before I leave, I invite Charlie to meet me in Portland for the party that night. "I mean, you know, if you want. A bunch of my old college friends have driven up together from California; we'll probably end up at that party tonight."

Until Rabbit started tap-dancing on top of the broken pay-phone booth outside the restaurant, I felt as if we were all pretty much under control. After the waiter came out of Montage, the late-night diner where had eaten, to tell him, "If you don't get down, I'm calling the cops on all of you for real this time," we all got quiet, and those of us prone to introspection began to rethink the evening's events.

I could see how Charlie, not used to large gatherings of Johnston alums, must have felt overwhelmed. At the party, we had both drunk a potion that he brought down with him (Charlie said that it was weed distilled in Everclear, but it looked and tasted like swamp water), which had both heightened and muffled our senses. Now everything is loud and bright and smudged at the edges.

Frank, a former RA (we used the term *community coordinators*), clasps Charlie's hand and says:

"You know what, Charlie? You're all right. I like you. In fact, you know what I'm going to do for you? Just for you. Tonight, I grant you an honorary degree from the Johnston Center for Integrative Studies. I can do that, because my brother went there too and he's married to another Johnston alum and I even worked there. I have the power to grant honorary degrees. OK, so give me your hand."

"Dude. You're already holding my hand."

"Right. OK."

The guy gives Charlie's hand a firm shake. "I now proclaim you honorary Johnston!" The rest of us whoop and yell "Buffalooooo!" and slap Charlie on the back as he smiles bashfully.

We count eight different years of Johnston alums between the twelve of us, and then there's this guy who drove all the way from Seattle to hang out with me on New Year's

Eve. That he is the same guy whom I met ten years ago in the art room at Sacramento Country Day only proves that wheels are turning in a cosmic sense tonight.

Before we get kicked out of Montage, I'm playing with the candle on the table, passing my fingers over it and whisking them away until my friend Peter extinguishes it between his fingers, chirping, "All gone!" Someone at the other end of the table yells something about chocolate cake, and someone else gets into a tiff with one of the waiters, who turns around and yells, "Ice bath for table four!" Two bus boys, both carrying two pitchers each of ice water, arrive and pour our glasses. I lose track of Charlie. He's there across the table from me, and then he's not. I try his phone; no response.

I peek around outside the restaurant into the pouring rain, and I can't find him. I call his phone again; still no response. I can't remember where he parked the car. He left, really left. He's gone back to Seattle. It was all too much, too soon. *I* was too much, too soon. I can't cry around the New Year's revelers on the street, so I shuffle back to Montage.

"Charlie's gone," I say to Peter, resigned. "I can't find him."

161

"He probably just went to the bathroom."

"It's been a while."

"Let's not worry about it until we get back to the cars."

"How the fuck are we getting home?"

"Jennie's driving. Don't worry, she hasn't been drinking."

"Yeah, but there aren't enough cars."

"Cole, it's fine. Logistics are taken care of. Here."

He swipes a candle off a nearby table and places it in front of me. He waggles his fingers over the flame, almost touching it, calling out "whooo!" as if he's on a roller coaster until I start giggling.

We're waiting for the check when Charlie unceremoniously sits back down at the table.

"Hey."

"Hey, I thought you headed back to Seattle!"

"Yeah. Sorry. That green stuff was too much for me. I had to sit in my car and listen to some Zappa to calm down."

I go silent.

"I'm sorry, I was just really overwhelmed."

"Here's what I'm not understanding."

I hesitate.

"Who the fuck listens to Frank Zappa to calm down?"

162

We both crack up.

How and when do you decide that you can trust someone?

Here is what I deduce about Charlie: He's a good person, a slightly sad person; whatever happens, he won't really hurt me intentionally. He probably won't reject me; at least not tonight. In the physical pain that his back causes him, he too has an invisible experience rooted in his anatomy that colors everything he does.

I'm already engaging in the cognitive dissonance that is essential to falling in love. If I remember now that good people have been hurting good people unintentionally from the beginning of time, that that is essential to being in a relationship, that I've hurt and been hurt by well-intended people more often than I've been hurt by sadists, then I would never date again.

The morning after New Year's Charlie and I are sitting at breakfast in the Doug Fir Lounge, the restaurant connected to the Jupiter Hotel in Portland designed to look like a combination log cabin and 1970s swingers club. "I can't move to Southern California for you," he says. "But there's this graduate program in Santa Barbara I've been looking into. It's like computer stuff mixed with art."

I look down into my coffee cup and roll my eyes. This is a ridiculously premature conversation. I don't so much date as fall into entanglements. I don't have any idea *how* to date. In entanglements the only certainty is that one person or the other will be let down, but the advantage over relationships is that this will happen quickly, rather than slowly.

When I get back to Valencia, Charlie starts calling me every night. On Valentine's Day, he sends me the dress that I was thinking about buying to wear to his sister's wedding. I've never been courted in a straightforward manner before. It's bewildering and overwhelming, and I'm most afraid that it will stop; so I try to stop it first. I write him an email telling him that I can't financially afford to be in a long-distance relationship, but his phone calls don't stop and I don't stop answering them.

In March, he asks me to come stay with him in Seattle for the summer, and then later that week he takes it back. A play that I wrote is being produced in a festival at school, and he visits to come see it. That summer I visit him in Seattle for a few days. A few days become a week, a month, and then a couple of months, until the summer is almost over.

One especially hot August afternoon, we dangle our legs off the edge of his loft bed and try to have a conversation about what it is that we're doing. It's warmest in the loft, but it's also closest to the fan that he's tied to the ceiling.

"In software development, there's this phase called *beta testing.* It's the transitional stage where we work out the bugs before taking the software public. Let's consider this summer beta testing."

The difference between relationships and software is that relationships are continually in transition. You can spend a lifetime, if you are lucky, trying to work the bugs out with another person.

Over the summer, Charlie and I become immersive foreign exchange students in each other's worlds of neurosis. He has systems and measurements for everything. Laundry: first the quarters go in and then, before starting the machine or putting the clothes in, the lint tray is cleaned. Never clothes before lint tray; this is incorrect. A single tiny dot of soap on the sponge for washing dishes, no more and no less. He does everything, from mixing drinks to fixing up his bike, with delicate precision. Every day, he wears jeans and the kind of black T-shirt purchased in packs of five at a big chain store. His world is like science fiction to me; I am fascinated. I measure everything in drips and splashes. My wardrobe is not generally described as either understated or consistent.

This is a symbiotic relationship. I am the little bird on the back of the hippo, cleaning his ears. I am leeching off Charlie's understanding of the spatial world. When we hold hands crossing the street, we look just like any other couple holding hands and crossing the street. There is a certain gentleness, what I can only describe as a quietly good-hearted feeling, to this relationship that I have not experienced before.

At the end of the summer, Charlie gives notice at his job at Boeing. In September, he will start his MS at the Science and Media Arts program at UC Santa Barbara.

It takes about an hour and a half to get to Valencia from Santa Barbara. It takes some money and courage; when Charlie visits me in graduate housing almost every weekend, I do my best to dole out what little I have of both. He tells me that my room assignment this year is a reflected mirror image of my room last year — the unmovable furniture that was on one side of the room last year is on the other side this year —

166

and though I don't recognize this myself, I believe him. I set the room up by myself this year and can't get over the eerie feeling that everything I've touched — my mirror, my printer, my books, my clothes — leans a little to the right.

I am terrified. At any moment, the trapdoor will open, ticker tape will fall from the sky, and horns will sound and lights will flash and the man with the cardboard check will come out to announce that this is the millionth time that I misplaced my trust in someone. I keep writing giant cardboard checks with my heart that my head refuses to cash.

September 2008
Valencia, California

As part of the program, I'm a teaching assistant for an introduction-to-writing course. Half of the MFA students are placed in charge of their own classrooms in support of a series of lectures given by a professor, the other half shadow different professors in their classrooms. Learning to teach is the main reason that I wanted to get my MFA, so I'm ecstatic and terrified to be one of the MFA students with my own classroom. All of my life, following the leader has been my biological imperative. In addition to navigating physical geography by playing a covert game of "follow the leader," I have also always watched and taken cues from my teachers and professors. The women who were my college professors were my guides to how a woman can be smart and funny and curious about the world and be completely, unapologetically, herself. Now, for the first time in my life, I'm expected to lead. My introduction-to-writing students are surly from the start, though I don't blame them for their lack of enthusiasm for five-paragraph essay structure.

Every Tuesday, the professor for this undergraduate course lectures on a different period of avant-garde art history, beginning with the futurists and ending with the conceptual artists of the late twentieth century. Every Wednesday, I meet with a cluster of students for ninety minutes to go over the lecture and to assign writing assignments concerning each art period. In addition to leading conversations and exercises in relation to the lecture sessions, I go over how to structure an essay, cite sources, and write a bibliography.

I make it up as I go along, artlessly lobbing different pedagogical tactics: joking, cajoling, threatening. I feel less like a teacher and more like a basketball coach in an uplifting sports movie, taking my ragtag team of colorful underdogs all the way to the pennant.

Some days, inevitably, are better than others. Some days I even get the sense that I know what I'm doing; those days feel like a homecoming. As overwhelmed as I am by the brain's potential to unravel, I am more moved by its elasticity.

WRITING ARTS: TWENTIETH-CENTURY ART MOVEMENTS AND SOCIETY SYLLABUS

COURSE #: CS110

Course Description

In the Wednesday discussion section of this course, we will be focusing on the twentieth-century avant-garde art movements presented in the lecture period and polishing our essay-writing skills by writing about certain works and artists of the era. You will be assigned three critical essays throughout the course of the semester. I will update you on paper topics, guidelines, and formatting as the first assignment approaches. You will be expected to turn in a rough draft as well as a revision of each piece.

Critical Studies Department Policies

Plagiarism Policy: As discussed in Professor Nelson's original syllabus, CalArts has a zero-tolerance policy when it comes to plagiarism; possible consequences of suspected plagiarism include failure in class and expulsion from the school. Plagiarism is identified as misrepresentation of someone else's work as your own.

(I am the only plagiarist here, the fake, the phony, standing in front of the twelve of you as if I know what I'm doing because I have a syllabus, a cup of coffee, and a blazer. I look like the real thing, but inside I can't believe that I'm getting away with this. The worst part is, I'm falling in love with teaching, so I hope that I'm never found out.)

Absences: You receive three absences, both in Professor Nelson's lecture and my class section. It is especially important that you be aware of your absences, as this class can only be retaken for your mandatory graduation credit at a community college over the summer.

Reading: The reader may be purchased at www.universityreader.com. I expect you to buy this reader ASAP and bring it to class every week. Reading should be completed before lecture on Tuesday, in order to get the most out of the week's lecture.

Grading: (How am I going to do this? The organizing, the rubric — don't let them smell fear; keep a calm and steady grip. Show authority, not vulnerability. They don't need to know. Nobody needs to know. Hide, reveal, retreat.) Check marks for handing in a three-by-five card with three questions: two from reading and one from lecture. Check marks for participation, for attendance. Check marks for having a thesis statement, for MLA formatting, a proper citations page. Data collected via check marks make up your paper grade as well as your ultimate grade.

Goals: I have been collecting blazers from Goodwill for years in anticipation of becoming a teacher. If I try to open the door with the hand that is also holding my coffee, make the wrong amount of copies or staple them backward, if I forget simple words mid-sentence and ask for the class's help, may I please remind you: I got this. I know all of your names, I researched discussion topics and prepared lectures. I will work harder than you will ever know.

Outcome: You will learn things you didn't know before; you will be challenged. For ninety minutes twice a week I will be a conduit instead of a charge.

October 2008
Valencia, California

All of the students have impossible expectations for the CalArts Halloween party. We've all heard the story about Paul Reubens passing out on the lawn, about the beer laced with hallucinogens. I'm dressed in a Harlem Globetrotters cheerleader uniform from the 1970s and a grotesque rubber mask of a chicken that I picked up at a toy store in Seattle. I tell inquirers that I'm a "party fowl." The mask is incredibly hot, and I can only see through holes in the beak, which creates the effect of watching the party through a telescopic lens. When the girl before me in the crushing line for drinks drops a beer on herself, an art student dressed as a giant box of tissues mops her up before disappearing back into the swarm of the party.

Feeling overwhelmed by the crowd, I

retreat with a few other writing students to the concrete hut at the end of the campus that houses our program. We're all acutely aware that our thesis defenses are only days away, but tonight is supposed to be about forgetting. Very few of the male writing students have dressed up this year. The man I'm sitting next to, a new student whom I haven't talked to much outside of class, is in his street clothes, a baseball cap jammed backward on his head.

I've noticed how authoritatively he remarks on other students' work in class; every so often his feedback is stalled by a stutter. When he gets stuck on a word, I feel ashamed because I don't know where to put my eyes. Blankly watching him stuck looping a syllable until his body allows him to right himself feels as though I'm adding pressure to the situation. I want to be able to help somehow, to run behind him and Heimlich the words out of him. I usually look down at my desk and wait.

I know what it is to be angry with your uncooperative body. Your body will inevitably fail you — if not now, then later. We are all lurching meat marionettes, Frankenstein monsters stitched together from stronger parts and weaker parts. Try to think of this as a happy thing, a joyful coltish clumsiness born of enthusiasm to be in the world.

I've taken off my chicken mask to facilitate drinking. He also has a beer in his hand.

"So, what's your thesis project?" he asks me, making polite party conversation.

"Yeah, I don't want to talk about that right now."

"You can tell me."

"Ask me tomorrow."

"No, no, tell me, what is it?"

"I don't want to talk about it."

Talking about my thesis sucks all the air out of the room; it's a conversation stopper, not exactly party chatter. But he persists, so I tell him, certain that afterward he will back off immediately.

"I have a hole in my brain. I'm writing about that."

"Well, I suppose I should congratulate you on being able to dress yourself, then."

He's smirking. This is a joke.

I look around the small room, which has grown quiet. One girl sitting on the floor in the corner awkwardly plays with the brim of her witch hat. The students are waiting to see if the man and I are going to fight, but I'm stunned into silence. I had assumed that he and I were somehow on the same team, this imaginary team of people who are forced to play the hand they're dealt, instead of two individuals who barely know each other.

The next day, unbeknownst to me, one of my friends in the program tells him that he needs to apologize to me. He does, in a very thorough and touching email.

The Thursday after the party, I will have to defend my thesis proposal by sitting in front of my class of twenty-five students and a panel of professors and discussing my process, my intentions. In trying to practice how I would answer their questions, I only come up with more of my own.

When I trip and fall, is that also when you would trip and fall? When I am certain that the car heading toward me will hit me, is it a justifiable fear? Do you drop your keys? Does a cup fall from your hand as often it falls from mine? Which hand? How often? Please record. When I feel comfortable in my body, is that the comfort you feel in yours? Because feeling comfortable in my body never feels the way I think it should feel.

On Thursday evening, I am scheduled to be the first to present my thesis proposal after break. During the break, I head to the water fountain, where I swallow a muddy rainbow of herbal anti-anxiety pills with names both beautiful and meaningless to me: rhodiola, cordyceps, taurine.

My adviser grips the skinny microphone and flashes a fiberglass smile in a sharkskin suit and shiny black dress shoes. *Now it's time to play a game!* The studio audience shuffles in from break. I take my seat and place my hand above the buzzer. The topics on the board include: "Is That Why You're Such a Bitch in Workshop?" "Are You Going to Publish This, or Is It Just Therapy?" and "Is It Fatal?" A hand goes up.

"So, is this, like, specific to you?"

"Yes."

"I mean, are you, like, the only person who has this?"

I explain that it's like stroke damage; each stroke results in a uniquely devastated neurological system. I didn't have a stroke, but what I have is unique to me, and I have not been able to find anyone else, via my Web research, with a hole filled with cranial fluid where the right parietal should be.

Another hand goes up.

"I just can't believe it's the size of a lemon. I mean, a *lemon*."

She pumps her fist in the air repeatedly, as you do when you pass a truck and you want the driver to blow the horn. I fail to decipher this motion, either some sort of call to arms or act of solidarity, or she's going to shake me down for my lunch money after class. I nod and thank her.

A hush falls over the class, signaling the end of the questions. I am thanked by my adviser and dismissed. Afterward, I go out with friends from class to an aggressively festive chain restaurant, where we drink everything there is to drink in every shape of glass there is made to hold it: a fishbowl, a volcano, a hurricane.

Come on, it's not that bad. You're really milking this, aren't you? This is really more of a *self-esteem* issue. I remember that one time when I said "left" and you went left, when I asked you for change and you counted it out, when I pointed to a clock and you nodded, when we lost the car and you found it, when I was feeling down and you kept patting me on the back. This is a bit much, isn't it? Don't you think this is really a bit much? Really. I hang out with you all the time, and *this*, this is bullshit, this is a lie, you are a liar, this is all fake, and you, well, obviously You Are a Fraud.

(I'm afraid of what my friends will say. I'm afraid that they won't believe me.)

February 2009
Redlands, California

The word *nostalgia* was originally a medical diagnosis. In the eighteenth century, nostalgia was diagnosed as a physical illness afflicting people who'd left the homeland that their body had grown accustomed to. *Pathopatridalgia. Patho,* the Latin root meaning "suffering"; *patri,* meaning "land of the father." From Latin to Greek, the root becomes *nostos,* "returning home," and *algos,* "pain."

Is this the pain of yearning for home or the pain of returning home? Nostalgia is a masochistic twinge, a need akin to wobbling the rickety tooth in your mouth in order to sort through the pain. *Yep, still hurts. Damn, I should get this checked out. Maybe tomorrow it will feel better; maybe if I just leave it alone.* But you are absently worrying that wobbly tooth again without meaning to or

180

thinking about it. It feels inexplicably good. Without meaning to or really thinking about it, you can find yourself jostling around your past for no good reason, not knowing what you are looking for. An old record, a meal at a familiar restaurant, a message from out of the blue, and there you are; twisting and contorting to get closer to the pain, to try to figure out its nature and origins, its roots. Diagnosis is a systematic labeling, an identification. Over time, the meaning of *nostalgia* has shifted from something solid — a diagnosis rooted in place — to something much more abstract: a yearning rooted in time.

"What are you doing next week?" I ask Charlie.

Valentine's Day is embedded in the coming week, but I don't ask, "What do you want to do for Valentine's Day?" or, worse, "What are we doing for Valentine's Day?"

That would imply that I cared, that we cared, about such things. Valentine's Day encompasses everything that I am trying not to be. It's a needy, soppy, expectant, frilly holiday; a pink codependent holiday, and I am a blue independent woman.

"Well, there's this concert, and Robert's going to be unveiling this robot he built to sing along to 'Suck My Giant Robot Dick,' and it has, like, this gigantic phallus that goes up and down while he sings. It's going to be awesome. I don't know if I'd be able to pick you up from Valencia in time fo—"

"Dude. You cannot leave me alone on Valentine's Day for a giant robot phallus."

"Oh. OK. Why, what's up?"

"The Johnston reunion is that weekend. I was wondering if you'd want to go with me?"

"To your college reunion with you?"

"Yeah."

"Oh, man, I don't know. That sounds . . . intense."

"Peter will be there; you love Peter. And Kristy and Matt — I mean Maddie."

The Johnston reunion, which is held once every five years in Redlands and welcomes everyone from any class dating back to 1976, happens to fall in my second year of grad school. Valencia is only a couple of hours from Redlands by car. I am bringing Charlie to silently ask for my little community's blessing; I need him to meet Maddie. Although I can't admit it to myself at the time, what I'm really saying by dragging my long-term boyfriend to my five-year college reunion is "Look at me! Here I am, five years after college graduation and finally in a stable relationship! I must be doing something right. I must be an adult now."

Maddie, whom I dated on and off during college, is one of the people I'm most looking forward to seeing. Maddie is the convex to my concave: extroverted, outgoing, a social butterfly. Still, we were unmistakably a pair, both curious and brutally impatient. Together, we sledded down the concrete stairs of our dorm on couch cushions and broke into the school church in the middle of the night to play the organ, nothing especially new in the world of college hijinks, but we felt we were inventing the world.

Maddie was the first person I had called about my brain. She said, "You mean this whole time *that's all it was*?" As if it was so simple, which somehow made me feel much better. A year later she called me right after she got her first estrogen shot.

She and I are both coming back to Johnston with different bodies, bodies truer to our selves. Mine is a secret self, hidden like a blister in a shoe. Maddie's transformation is external and highly public, Matt to Maddie. Our only sameness is that our new bodies are rooted in a physical and emotional history that was incongruent with our external selves.

I don't presume to know what Maddie's

transition is like for her; I do know a little about being the unwilling captive of a body that performs a pantomime of fulfilling the expectations of others. I have loved a pantomime of her body when we dated in college, watched those shoulders slope in sleep.

Maddie dresses like a punk-rock Frida Kahlo in skirts sewn together in thick, bold railroad-track stitches, feathers and plastic flowers in her hair. She has breasts, hips, and a new tattoo on her inner forearm, a Russian nesting doll. Stacking selves within selves — it's what we've all done in the five years since we graduated from Johnston.

Right now her voice still has the same deep tone that it had when we were in college, but her inflections have started to change, twisting the periods that used to end each sentence into question marks. Eventually, the tone of her voice will also change.

Several of us are staying at the Stardust Motel, a collection of run-down rooms that's not without its charms, one being that it is in drunken stumbling distance from campus; another being the avocado rotary phones and the framed paintings of unicorns on the wall that look like they were ripped out of children's drawing books.

All of our bodies have changed, of course. Some of us are fatter, and fewer of us are thinner; some have less hair, and some stopped shaving. A few have had babies — one woman who lives in Redlands brings her two young children and husband. My last vivid memory of her prior to the reunion is of when she was tripping on mushrooms, hanging herself out the third-floor dorm window in a hot-pink bikini crying and screaming and threatening to jump, while several people grabbed her by the arms and waist to try to pull her back inside.

A few of us assemble at the house of our former writing professor for some tea and biscuits and to catch up and play with her dogs. As I leave the party, Maddie pulls me in for a hug good-bye and whispers in my ear, "I like him. He's a sweetheart."

■ ■ ■ ■

IV.
ARRIVAL

■ ■ ■ ■

"I can't explain myself, I'm afraid, Sir," said Alice, "because I'm not myself, you see."
— Lewis Carroll, *Alice in Wonderland*

May 2009
Valencia, California
I am here to collect.

As the star of my own vengeful action thriller, *The Claimant,* I want my identity back, someone's head on a platter for making me wait twenty-seven years to find out who I am, someone else's head on a platter for how little this new information about me actually *changes* me. I want your help, and I want nothing to do with you. I am The Claimant.

I'll be graduating from my MFA program in a month, and while I feel both a bit of relief and perhaps even some validation now that I know why I was such a bad fit at my postcollege jobs, I don't know where this leaves me now, other than unfit for the same jobs that I assumed that I'd return to after finishing my MFA.

I try to think of applying for Social

189

Security as a temporary stopgap measure that allows me to remain independent while figuring out where I fit into the workforce. More than anything, I want to teach writing, but I know that those positions are hard to come by even in the best of times. Even if I wasn't graduating in a recession, it's rare for anyone coming straight out of an MFA program to go straight into teaching. The MFA is a studio degree, giving us time to work on our writing and practice teaching for the first time. After graduation, some of us will go on to PhD programs; some of us will adjunct at community colleges; most of us will go back to the jobs we had before we took two years to focus on writing. I don't know what I'm going to do after graduation. Charlie doesn't want me to move in with him in Santa Barbara, and I don't want to go back to my parents' house in Portland. I've been putting out some feelers with friends who live in the Bay Area, but if this claim doesn't go through I'll have to go back to my parents'.

It didn't occur to my family at first that I might be eligible for Social Security, but my father had a conversation about me with a student of his who has a heart condition. The student suggested that we look into it. Even with his help, it took a year to find our way through the byzantine coding system that I would have to fit into in order to be recognized as officially disabled.

It takes me several drafts to fill out my Social Security paperwork.

1. Name of disabled person (First, Middle, Last)
   NICOLE FREDI COHEN
2. Social Security number
   084-92-3656
3. Date (month, day, year)
   5/27/09
4. Your daytime telephone number
   (503) 697-4499

Describe what you do from the time you wake up until going to bed.

- Wake up
- ~~Drink pots of coffee (2–3)~~
- Eat breakfast
- ~~Pretend to self and others that we can help each other become "better writers." Try not to think too hard about this.~~
- Go to class
- ~~Think about this too hard~~
- ~~Avoid cafeteria (crowds, lines, inevitable spilling, too many options) at all costs~~
- ~~Eat hummus~~

- Eat lunch
- ~~Glare at pile of reading for school~~
- ~~Check email~~
- ~~Consider writing a poem in the hopes of concluding global issues~~
- ~~Miss parents' cats~~
- Study/write
- ~~Eat hummus~~
- Eat dinner
- ~~Sneer with judgment at own bookshelf~~
- ~~Watch TV~~
- ~~Take off headphones~~
- Go to bed

In interpreting my daily tasks as official government business, I see how much extra time it takes for me to complete mundane chores. The organizational ritual of hanging up and organizing fresh laundry, for example — making sure that all of the clothes are hung facing the same direction, placing like with like; it takes me a lot of time, and I have to really force myself to do it. After my parents and I figure out the paperwork together and send it in, we wait to hear anything. I am categorized under "Impairments, Mental," as subscribing to the subcategories (of which you must pick at least two) "Marked restriction in activities of daily living" and "Marked difficulties in maintaining concentration, persistence, or pace." It's difficult for me to consider myself someone with a mental impairment — I was raised in a family that values intellectual curiosity above all else — but if I learned anything in Dialectical Behavior Therapy, it's that strength and weakness share a home in the head.

The woman who calls me for my Social Security interview has no first name. She does not exist outside of this phone call.

"This is Mrs. Dixon. I'm going to ask you a series of questions to confirm for me what you've written here on these forms for us."

"OK."

She is stiff and formal with me; I mimic her intonations. Mirroring is a simple and highly effective coping mechanism for blending in, one that comes automatically to me. This is how I ace interviews for jobs that I could never possibly maintain. Appearing competent, putting on the verbal version of a suit and tie, is one of my favorite things to do because I *feel* competent when I do it and am thus temporarily treated as such. I get the job, and it's not until an average of three months later, when I've flipped the numbers while jotting down an important phone message again, or miscalculated the final total from behind a cash register and have to ring you up a fourth time as you are calling for my manager, that my incompetence is unmasked.

This interview is for the job of being disabled, and yet still I'm masking, trying to appear as "together" as possible. I have no idea what is expected of me here or how to be that person. I'm new here; even though I've never been anyone else. As a professional mime, taking my social cues from someone else, I don't know how to interview for the job of being myself. Mrs. Dixon asks me to verbally certify that everything I say is the truth, and she is explicit about how everything that I say is legally binding in that if the federal government thinks that I am lying, I could go to jail and/or they could make me pay back any Social Security that I am granted.

All of her basic and straightforward questions about dates and time are exactly the kind that I have never been able to answer. I have a copy of my paperwork out in front of me with the amount I make in a month, in a year, and the dates I have worked. This is my script, not to be deviated from. Mrs. Dixon did not get this memo, however, because she keeps asking me questions that are not covered in my papers, forcing me to improvise.

"How many hours a week did you work at Vowel?"

"Ummm . . . I'm not sure . . . Can you hold on for a moment, please?"

I flip through the forms. The answer is not in here. How could it not be in here? I must be missing it. I flip through again; I can't find it. I will have to say *something.* How many hours a week is it normal to say that I worked? Barring any knowledge of the correct answer, what is a proper guess? Eighty hours? Sixty? I worked part-time, so would it be more like fifteen? Thirty? How many hours generally pass from when I walk to my desk with a cup of coffee in the morning and when I break for lunch? I have absolutely no recollection. My brain doesn't hold on to hours. I don't understand calculating days in blocks of time. I understand "a long time" and "a short time," although these concepts are constantly reversing and backing up on each other, since what feels like a long time can be a short time and vice versa. I would guess that I worked half a day at Vowel. Don't ask me how long that is.

"How much were you paid?"

I answer straight from the paper in my hand while moving my finger over the numbers as a safeguard against flipping them, a commonplace act that in this moment could forever place me erroneously in a higher or lower tax bracket.

I practiced beforehand by reviewing the paperwork several times, but in the moment I'm so nervous and flustered that I can't find the answers on the paper. I want to say: "I don't know, OK? I don't know what I made or how long I worked. I show up at a certain time, take lunch at a certain time, and then I go home. I get a check for that time; I put it in the bank. Just like you, I sleepwalk through these things without memory. Unlike you, I cannot fill in these blanks with assumptions. I don't have that repository to draw from, how much I must have worked and how much I must have made. I have no idea. And that, Mrs. Dixon, is exactly why I am on the phone with you." Instead, I shuffle my papers and try my very best to give the right answers, feeling confused and utterly helpless.

"I see . . . and how long have you had these symptoms for?"

"Uuuuuh . . . since June of last year."

Is that right? Is that what she means? I have had this condition my entire life, but I have had *this*, this information, this diagnosis, this picture of a hole in my head, since last summer. No wait, that's not right. It was the summer before last, when I was living in Portland in the key lime–colored house with the couple and their two cats, before the one in Seattle with Charlie's fifty Speak & Spells. I am like a wind-up toy; placed down with the key cranked up and the motor spinning, I loop my way through months without direction, spitting out tiny sparks, crashing a pair of cymbals. I get turned around, picked up out of time, and placed back in a new hour or a new day or month or year, that easily.

I know the order of days in a week, but I have a hard time with the order of months in a year and an especially difficult time matching the name of a month with its assigned numerical order. I write out the names of months on checks and papers for school because I often write the incorrect numerical date. I try to ride time out, follow the structure of hours and days and months set before me, but I'm constantly thrown off and scrambling to get back on again.

The only way to place myself in time is through narrative, through telling myself the story of my life over and over. The summer of my diagnosis was the summer when I terrified myself by actually getting into grad school, which was both better and worse than the summer before that, the summer when I terrified myself by not getting in.

By the end of our conversation, I'm certain that I have just flunked an interview for the job of being myself.

"You told her *what*? Call her back! Right now!" A soft-spoken librarian who spends her days wrapped in a cocoon of hushing, my mother is by nature not a screamer. It's well known in our family, however, that if she's yelling at you, you're pretty much a goner. The most common mistake my sisters and I make is being the first to shout. But I hadn't yelled!

I repeat myself, quietly, fearfully, "I told her I've had this since June of last year."

"You call her back right now and explain that you were *born* with this! You were only *diagnosed* in June 2007!"

I weave my way through the departmental phone tree and punch in Mrs. Dixon's extension and anxiously speed through my clarification.

"Hi. I'm sorry, I just have to explain — I was born with this. I have had these . . . difficulties since birth, but I had my MRI last June. Not this past June — the one before it. So I've had this my entire life. But I just found out about it in June 2007."

"Oh. OK. Thank you. I am sure that is already clear in your files. But thank you for calling and clarifying."

I call back my mom, who by now has returned to a more characteristically calm tone.

"I'm sorry; I'm sorry that I yelled. It's just that you've worked so hard for this, and I don't want it to get messed up *now.*"

I've worked so hard for this? There is an understanding now in my family that all of my previous testing, all of my mistaken diagnoses and the confusing prescriptions, all of the awkward shame of being mislabeled and misunderstood by both others and myself, were all time clocked in. The story of my neurological life is spelled out in those therapist's blocks making up a pattern that I fumble to put together. Everyone's life is a puzzle made up of infuriating patterns invisible to us, yet so painfully obvious to those who love us.

June 2009
Portland, Oregon

Once you've had one medical test with shocking results, no test is routine. Each one is a booby trap looking to sucker-punch you with some new insight into your mortality. Fear the stethoscope; become wary of the blood pressure cuff, suspicious of the stirrups. These tools, once your allies in preventative medicine, are now implicit in your demise. The only thing to do is to take off your hospital gown, put your pants back on, and go home to wait by the phone for that sharp snapback on the leash of your lifeline.

I am on the plane to Portland for the weekend, to return to CalArts on Monday. The Department of Social Security has requested that I submit to an optometry exam while it's deliberating on my disability claim. Disability is ultimately a federal claim, but you begin by filing a claim in your state. Since my neurologist and neurological chiropractor are both in Portland, it makes the most sense for me to file in Oregon. My understanding of the circumstances surrounding this test is that whoever examined my file was not convinced that my condition is neurological. How you could look over my MRI results and come to the conclusion that the issue is with my eyes is beyond me. I doubt that I'm the one in need of vision testing, but I have no choice.

I'm feeling especially nervous about how my sisters will react to my visit.

My sisters and I have a joke we make when we greet each other after an extended absence. We hug and pat each other on the back, saying, "I'm hugging you, but I'm hitting you." I don't remember how it started, but it's an analogy for our relationship, for the tenderness and brutality of sibling lives. It's also another example of how the tension behind genuine moments in our family is diffused by a joke.

The night that Carly was born, my dad took me out for Chinese food. At dinner, I bit and scratched him and screamed so loudly that we were thrown out of the restaurant. Before Marni was born, Carly and I were required by our parents to attend a preparatory class at the hospital in New Jersey where she would be born. In the class, the hospital gave us pink pins proclaiming I'M A BIG SISTER! and we colored in pictures of fathers happily changing diapers. Twenty years later, we are still not prepared for Marni. We call Carly the white sheep of the family, as she was the only one of the sisters who ever made any effort to conform. Marni says that she's most like our father "because I'm crazy," and Carly says that she's most like our mother because they share chameleon-like tendencies. Maybe I am the gray sheep, split between my black sheep father, who left the orthodoxy and his entire family to look for answers in philosophy, and my quiet white sheep mother, who worked in the library and hid behind a camera to make her art.

When I first heard of Marni's piece about me for her college memoir class, entitled "Genius or Dunce," my mom told me over the phone, "Let me just read you the end."

"No, Mom, just — no."

"Come on, let me just tell you about it! It's not so bad! OK, so Carly and Marni are in the car, and Carly is driving. Carly turns to Marni and says, 'You know, you and Cole might get along. You're both weird.' And Marni ends the piece with her saying 'Maybe.' "

"Touching."

Since then, I've read it in its entirety several times, and I'm trying to just sit with my responsibility for the anger steaming off her pages. Carly was already living in her own apartment when I graduated from college, but Marni was still living at home for the worst of my postcollegiate/prediagnosis swan dive. I was living in the house in Southeast with a rotating cast of roommates, but I was in such rough shape that more often than less I ended up at my parents'. At best, it's embarrassing to be the oldest sister who hasn't quite got a handle on skills for living on her own, while no one, including you, knows what the hell is wrong with you. At worst, I worry that the screaming fits and suicidal ideation that punctuated this period of my life, that took over our lives as a family, permanently marred any chance I have at a relationship with my sisters.

Marni is an eloquent writer.

They say that if you put two fists together, fingers folded, pressed in, and the bottom of your palms touching, it makes the size of your brain. Imagine the left pointer finger, middle finger, and thumb missing. Just fluid where they ought to be. That was the inside of Nicole's head. . . . For a while, we tried to figure out how someone could be born without part of their brain. No one had any answers. We weren't doctors. And doctors had never seen this before.

"Yeah, well, I thought you were faking too," Carly told me offhandedly on the phone when I called her to see if she'd read Marni's piece about me. "Then I saw the picture, and I thought, *Holy crap, I'm an asshole.*" We both started giggling.

Marni wrote that Carly always felt like the oldest sister to her. Though we never spoke of it, I am not surprised to read this. When they saw my behavior as a performance, their anger was justified. Now that we know that I have a real physical condition, the anger that was already simmering becomes a complex stew of resentment over a situation that we are all powerless to change. As the source of it all, I have always found it difficult to locate the proper vantage point from which to assess the damage I've caused my younger sisters. This damage was no easier for me to decipher sitting in front of my computer in Valencia, reading Marni's essay, than it was when we were all under the same roof in Davis, or will be when we reunite in Portland when I deboard this plane.

"Is Cole going to be there?" I had to ask. She could change the family dynamic so drastically, I wanted to know what kind of family dinner this would be.

Marni wrote of my time at CalArts.

She suggested I look into the school; "they have a program on puppetry you'd like." I promised to look into it. Haven't gotten around to it yet. Haven't gotten around to being her friend yet either.

There is a shadow family, one I don't belong to, living in Portland while I am not. Carly is the oldest, and Marni is the youngest. Because it's a family that collapses once I enter the room, it's one that I can never be part of. This is the natural consequence of my position as a priority in the familial triage of childhood. There are three of us and one oxygen mask, and I strapped it on first. I can't blame my sisters if they can't breathe whenever I'm home.

Part of me is looking forward to being back in Portland; it's always somewhat comforting to be back among so many people striving to be different in the same way. On the plane, I read music magazines and books for school and avoid any and all eye contact with the passenger next to me, lest this person attempt to converse with me. Out the window I watch the tan and brown desert plains of Southern California morph into the greens and blues of Oregon.

"Folks, this is your captain. Looks like we've got about thirty minutes until the seat-belt sign goes on and stays on as we head into PDX, so if you'd like to head to the bathroom or stretch your legs one last time before we begin our descent, now would be the time. *Aaaand* if you take a look over through your right passenger-side window, you'll notice the Three Sisters, the trio of volcanic peaks, one of the natural wonders Oregon is known for. You're looking at the third-, fourth-, and fifth-highest peaks in Oregon, right over there on your right. Little history lesson, here, folks, bear with me. That top one, the North Sister, is the oldest of the three, with towering rock pinnacles and glaciers. Don't worry, it hasn't erupted since the late Pleistocene, over a hundred thousand years ago, people, and it's considered extinct. We've got some packets of peanuts back here with a similar expiration date. But seriously, folks, it is the most dangerous climb of the Three Sisters, due to its level of erosion, and thus rockfall. North Sister, Nicole Cohen, often referred to as Cole, is also prone to mood swings, insomnia, fluctuations in weight, and an abbreviated attention span. So if you're thinking of taking a hike during your stay in Oregon, this one's best left to the professionals.

"Middle Sister, Carly Cohen, is the smallest, at five feet four inches, and the most poorly studied. It is also the middle in age. Middle Sister is a stratovolcano consisting primarily of basalt but also erupted andesite, dacite, and rhyodacite. Middle Sister is also known for affection for young adult literature and the sale section at J. Crew or, preferably, Anthropologie. No reports on its potential for eruptions have been made. Silent but deadly, folks, silent but deadly.

"South Sister, Marni Cohen, also known as Mo to locals here in Oregon, is a long, steep, nontechnical hike that can be easily completed in a day by reasonably fit hikers. This particular volcano is also known for its gigantic Jew-fro, which is studiously maintained, and a tendency toward sarcasm and adopting stray animals and roommates. Little-known fact: South Sister, while being quite thin itself, is situated above a thrift store specializing in clothing for plus-size ladies, located in the basement of the surrounding territory. Popular starting points are the Green Lakes and Devil's Lake trailheads. *Aaaand* that concludes our tour of Three Sisters, folks."

My father is the only one there to greet me at the airport, with our traditional family greeting. "Hey, it's Uncle Heshe!" he yells and waves his arms. This started when I first returned from college for breaks, and now it's been going on for so long that I'd be vaguely insulted if I didn't receive the proper familial airport greeting. We leave immediately for the giant Asian supermarket, where we eat at the food court without paying. I'm not sure if my father believes that because he teaches courses on ethics he transcends ethical obligations, or that teaching ethics justifies his personal obligation to subvert traditional concepts of justice and morality, such as paying for lunch. I tend toward feelings of affection for my father's spotty moral code, especially when it lands me free duck in chili sauce. Rule breaking makes for great father-daughter bonding.

We decide to check out the new aerial tram, a cross between a ski lift and a giant silver bean that glides over I-5 from the South Waterfront District to the hospital. Neither of us mentions that this is the first time that we've been back to this hospital together since he accompanied me for my MRI. As we glide over the pines and the tops of houses, I'm reminded of that PBS painting show that I used to draw along to with my crayons when I was little, the one where the smiling host with the scrub-brush hair encouraged his audience to paint "happy little trees." I grip the guide bar by the window. A man on his cell phone next to me is arguing with the person on the other end of the line about his health insurance. The ride is pretty short; not long after we leave the ground we're pulling into the shiny metal dock on the other side of the hospital.

"Let's get a coffee." Dad points out a coffee stand behind the glass hospital doors.

"What can I get you?" the woman behind the coffee cart asks.

"What can you *get me*?" my father asks back.

"What can I *get you*?" she asks again.

The woman smiles nervously, unsure if this is a game or if he's truly irate. This is how routine interactions with my dad usually begin.

"Are you making fun of my accent?" he asks.

"No, sir. Are you from New York?"

"No, I'm just putting this on for *you.*"

We walk around the hospital with our coffees, looking at the donated art.

"This morning, I asked my intro-to-ethics class what they did this weekend, and they just stared back at me like a bunch of morons, slouched over with their backward caps."

"Huh."

"So I said, 'Come on, you didn't do anything this weekend? Nobody saw a movie? Nothing?' and finally this one girl in the back raised her hand and I called on her and she said, 'Why would we tell you what we did this weekend? You're just going to make fun of us.'"

"So what did you say to that?"

"I explained to her that when someone from New York makes fun of you, it's a sign of affection."

"And how did that go over?"

"Nothing. They just stared at me."

I get together with Carly and Mo for drinks at a Tiki bar in Northeast. Over coconut-shaped cups with wheels of pineapple wedged on the brims, we don't talk about why I'm here or Mo's piece, but we agree to meet for "sister drinks" whenever I'm back in town. We never did this before my MRI, when we all lived in the same town. I think, I hope, that by moving away I've created some space for them. We still go to the same bar every time, where the dehydrated blowfish on the ceiling smile their frozen fanged grimaces and the stoic wide-mouthed Polynesian statues overhear our drunken confessions and spats. For all of our differences, we are united by umbrella drinks.

In the morning, my mother is taking me to Pacific University Medical Center for the eye exam. She will come into the exam room with me. Long ago, I found it much easier to let my mom join me in exam rooms rather than be peppered with a series of questions about why I didn't ask this or that or what the doctor said exactly. I can never answer these questions to my parents' satisfaction, and when they send me to an exam with a list of their questions, I usually forget to ask them or don't do a satisfying job of recounting the answers. Since the exam was ordered by someone in the Department of Social Security, my parents and I are both extra-anxious about how to behave.

The waiting room has two built-in couches, parallel from each other as if the patients are all in the same subway car. I can see my file already on the receptionist's desk as I check in for my appointment. I take a seat on the couch next to my mom and wait. It's 9:00 a.m., the place is empty. Every so often a different young man in a dress shirt and tie walks up to the reception desk, but there's a noticeable absence of white coats or the usual sense of urgency. "Intern Coter to the reception desk, Intern Coter." I realize that the young men I'm seeing are all medical interns. The young man who walks into the waiting room to call my name and shake my hand has pudgy cheeks and thickly gelled hair. His shirt is lavender, and his tie is purple, with a gradient of polka dots that eventually change color from dark purple, toward the knot, to light blue at the bottom of the tie. He looks more likely to sell me a car or a religion than to check my eyesight. He leads us to the exam room, where he asks me to read the letters on a variety of charts.

"Well, you've got twenty/fifteen vision. Better than twenty/twenty. So let's write in twenty/fifteen, just because we can . . ." I'm not sure if he's talking to me or to himself as he scribbles in my chart. "Now, let's test your peripheral vision." He walks me down the hallway toward a closed door. He opens the door, and inside are three more formally dressed men in their early twenties looking into a variety of giant lenses encased in white plastic. They look like 1950s high school students crowded around a chemistry set. These guys decide the fate of my disability claim? I take a deep breath and try to calm myself with thoughts of brunch afterward. My assigned intern is having a hard time getting the attention of the other ones. "Hey, guys? You guys, I have a *patient* in here? Are you here with a *patient*?" His strained professional tone makes the other junior optometrists scatter out of the exam room.

"OK." He turns back to me. "Have a seat right here, please." He gestures toward a stool as he fumbles around with some papers and instruments and darkens the room. "Wow, that is a terrible eye patch; let me get you a better one." The junior optometrist hands me an eye patch, which I place dutifully on one eye. I'm already sneering so the patch doesn't feel particularly out of place. "OK, now if you will just stick your head in here and rest your chin on the strap . . ." I turn around on the stool to face a white plastic half sphere, like the inside of a giant globe, with a little black cushioned bench toward the bottom for my chin. Still wearing the eye patch, I place my chin on the bench. The junior optometrist sits on the other side of the half globe, peering through a tiny pinprick lens in the center. I am trying to recall my geometry. Which is convex and which is concave? I decide that since concave has the word *cave* in it and my head is in a little head cave, my end must be concave.

Inside the head cave, my job is to follow a dot of yellow light with my eyes until I can't see it anymore. Whenever the dot enters or leaves my field of vision I am to click on the clicker in my hand, which appears to be wired to the globe but doesn't make any sound other than a quiet click when I press it with my thumb. After a while this gets boring. It's not long before I'm pretending to myself to be a chicken embryo floating inside an egg just to keep myself awake and entertained.

Afterward, the junior optometrist brings in the head optometrist, whom I can't help but think of as the daddy optometrist, certain that this is more a seminary or an orphanage than a medical center. I imagine the head optometrist lecturing on vision by day before doling out gruel to his charges before bed. The head optometrist reports that there's nothing wrong with my eyes. "You do have a shorter range of vision in your left eye, but in order to qualify for any kind of vision disability you'd have to have about twenty percent visibility left, which clearly you do not have. I recommend that you see a neurologist or someone in physical rehab."

This is the part that my mom has been waiting for, the postexam question-and-answer period.

"So why did they send us here?"

The optometrist looks at my file.

"Well, it looks like they sent this file to an optometrist, and he couldn't make a call because there was no previous eye exam on record. So they sent you for an eye exam." There was no previous eye exam because this is not an issue of my eyes as physical organs; this is an issue concerning my brain and the information it does or does not send me about what my eyes are seeing.

Let's say you're walking down a city street with a friend. Up in the sky, you see a big red balloon.

"Look!" you say to your friend, pointing.

"A balloon! Look!"

You point at the sky. But your friend does

not see the balloon. "Up there!" you cry. You point again, your finger following the balloon, but your friend does not see it. "Look, see, right there! By that building!" But your friend still does not see the balloon. "Look! Look!" You repeat the command and wave and point until you become exasperated. You are frustrated with your friend for not seeing what you see.

"This exists!" you are yelling, but if your friend doesn't see it, then obviously your friend cannot confirm it. My testimony is not what I witness but what I miss, a testimony of exasperation.

Teachers are exasperated with me for not understanding what they are trying to teach me; friends are exasperated with me for "playing dumb"; my parents are exasperated by scheduling and shuttling and reminding me; my sisters are exasperated by the attention I take up; strangers are exasperated when they give me basic directions and I ask them to repeat them and then I thank them and walk off to do the exact opposite of what they said; bosses are exasperated by training and retraining me for remedial tasks like filing or working a cash register.

"Look!" they are saying.

"Look! It's right here! Can't you see it?

Look closer! Harder! For God's sake, just *open your eyes and look*!"

I fill out new medical forms for every doctor or specialist I see. At Dr. Volt's, Dr. Z's, at the optometrist's office, I fill out new patient intake forms over and over again until my personal medical history begins to take on its own rhythm. The history of my body becomes a mantra chanted before each new doctor visit. My grandfather's colon cancer, my grandmother's breast cancer, my mother's thyroid disease, my father's high cholesterol. The conflicting moment when I choose, over and over again, to lie about my history of depression; the ritual of filling out forms is a ritual of taking stock of my body and the bodies of my family; past and present, alive and dead. I place a check mark where these bodies have failed themselves, a check mark where my body fails itself.

A doctor's chart is information about the body that's been gathered and organized for assessment. It is data used to confirm, to predict, to plot a course of action. But the narrative of my body has refused the traditional course of action of familiar hospital dramas. I walk out of each doctor's office with more information, data charted, but without a prescription, a cure, a recovery. I want desperately for someone to say, "Here, take this, you'll feel better." The story of diagnosis has two endings: recovery or death. Traditional medical narratives do not have much to tell us about coping.

At a certain point, the walls of each new waiting room begin to constrict like a swollen throat. I'm trying to assess for myself what I can heal and what I need to learn to live with, but the brain is tricky territory. Once we think we've mapped it, we slip down another new corridor. The path that we're certain is responsible for remembering how to ride a bike has a trapdoor that leads to memories of when your bike was stolen when you were seven. How will I know when I feel better? Will it happen gradually, or will my spatial world just shift into focus one day as I am out running errands? Just what is it that I'm looking for? And if I am cured, if I am healed — then who am I?

Two weeks after my eye exam in Portland, my pending Social Security claim concludes as it began, with another phone call from someone lacking a full name.

"Hi, Nicole? This is Pam. Your case has been reviewed, and they've agreed to grant you disability, but we don't believe that you should be placed in charge of the checks, so we'd like to put someone in charge of them for you."

I laugh. "Yeah, that's smart. That's a smart move."

Pam doesn't laugh. I wonder if she's bored, or if she's not allowed to laugh; she probably doesn't find my lack of basic math skills as funny as I do in this moment.

"Is there someone I can put in charge of these for you? Is there someone who handles your bills for you?"

"Um. Can I put two people?"

"No, you can only put one."

Choosing between two parents is a potential minefield. I go with my mother, whose name is already attached to my bank account because she wrote and sent out monthly checks for me when I lived in Portland. When I lived in Portland, I brought my monthly bills over to my parents' house, and my mother and I worked on them together. Left to my own devices, I have a hard time reading the bills and understanding how they came to a certain total, an issue that's exacerbated by my tendency to mail the wrong check to the wrong company without realizing it, resulting in mysterious double billings the following month. When I do it with someone else to double-check me, slow me down, and explain the charges, I can take care of my bills efficiently. On my own, I regularly end up in a quagmire of extra fees and phone calls to track down checks that I swear I mailed out on time. One of the great ironies of how I live is that to be a responsible adult I need help to take care of basic adult tasks.

On my own, I feel like a failure because my mangled attempts at flying solo only highlight over and over, with ridiculously consistent and vividly excruciating results, the basic things that I cannot do. I push back against taking responsibility for my weaknesses — by plunging head-on into a department store or concert hall where I will inevitably become lost, by sending out my own bills only to get double billed next month — because I want to believe that I can be like anyone else. I want to prove something by doing these things on my own. But for me, the key to becoming an independent adult is in learning to determine when a task is suitable for me and when it isn't, to know when it is appropriate to challenge my own understanding of my limitations and when I'm just getting myself into a bigger mess. It makes sense that I can't accept my own disability checks, but I still find it embarrassing. Pam calls my mother, who names my father as her backup.

"What do we do now?"

I'm on the phone with my friend Kristy, the first person I call with the news of my legal disability status. Most people get disability benefits as a result of a tragedy or a disfigurement or an illness. For me, nothing *happened.* Nothing changed. Now, nothing changing is changing my life in significant ways. I am finally becoming the person I have always been.

"Do we have a barbecue?"

"Cole, if they aren't trusting you with a check, I'm pretty sure you can't be trusted to hold a barbecue."

"Oh, right. I guess I'll just have to have my *mom* hold the barbecue *for* me."

I want some ritual to mark this transition into being. But nothing really happens. A couple of weeks later, my mom deposits the first check in my bank account, and slowly, over time, something starts to shift inside me, like a lens coming into focus.

For the first time, my perception is being validated. Someone sees what I see and shouts, "Yes, yes, there it is! Over there!" And still, until the phone call from Pam, it felt highly possible that my application for disability status would be rejected, ultimately negating my experience of the world. It felt possible that the federal government would call and say, "You're fine. Your father maybe didn't pay enough attention, and your mother maybe paid too much. It's not something to make a federal case of."

This isn't the worst of worlds by far, but it is my world, and even though you can't see it, I am going to ask you to believe in it. On the one hand, I hide in plain sight; I *pass*. On the other hand, I am doubted.

June 2009
Oakland, California

Graduating from CalArts after two years of classes and workshops is like scrambling out of a bomb shelter into the postapocalyptic rubble of a world populated by the undead. While we were ensconced in workshops debating the use of first-person plural, the rest of the country grappled with the 2008 financial crisis. As we crafted performative cut-up homages to Rrose Sélavy, people more in touch with current affairs — those who are losing their homes to impossible mortgages, who can't find jobs, those we are joining — are looking to mythical immortal creatures for entertainment and catharsis. Books and TV shows are all about vampires or zombies. What we want and what we are horrified by are often the same. We're both the bloodthirsty zombie who kills to feed and the hero who happens upon a crossbow in postapocalyptic lower Manhattan. We want to live forever, and we want to bash in the head of anyone who dares to live forever. Financial analysts are pointing out that sales of horror movies and lipstick are up. The only time that your biological impulses make it impossible to think about anything is when you're either terrified or orgasmic. Banks collapse, unemployment rises, the housing market crumbles. In 2009, we are all gasping for breath. I'm poking my head out of my art school bomb shelter, looking to run for cover. "MFA! Mother Fucking Artist!" the school of visual arts graduates chant as they walk up to the podium during the graduation ceremony. When so little is in your control, that's when you amp up the bravado.

I'm at an early graduation party when I get a text from my friend Jackie that someone in her cozy little building in downtown Oakland is looking for a new roommate. When she tells me that the building is just a few blocks from the Twelfth Street BART station and in walking distance to Chinatown, I jump at it.

I read in a guidebook that the weather in Oakland, California, is most similar to that of the Mediterranean, sunny and balmy beach weather. I've never been to the Mediterranean, but I feel safe in assuming that weather is the only condition that they have in common.

One month after graduating from CalArts, I'm in Oakland, three hundred miles away from Santa Barbara and Charlie, trying to make it work with my new roommate. I resolve to be optimistic about my living situation.

When I head up from Southern California with Peter, my friend from Johnston, to check the place out, I'm greeted coolly at the door by my would-be roommate, a blonde with a ragged pixie cut poking out from under some sort of straw lounge hat with a dark ribbon band; it's the kind of hat that makes me think of old Latin men chomping on cigars in Miami but seems to have been claimed by young white people. The hat is perched sideways on her head, complementing a vest covered with several gold chains. The pixie, Stacey, gives me a quick tour of the estate.

"If you flush the toilet, you need to wait ten minutes. So no courtesy flushes if you go number two, OK?" The place is immaculate, with wooden floors and a claw-foot bathtub. It looks like paradise compared to the six-person graduate housing apartment I recently fled.

"When my boyfriend lived here, this was our living room." She points to the empty room that I am here to stake a claim to. I nod empathetically. "Oh, he left these." She wanders to a small storage nook behind the kitchen. Two sets of beady, begging eyes look up at me from inside their cage. Rats. Rats and I have a complicated relationship. I am not disgusted or disturbed by them, but if I handle them I break into hives. *It should be fine as long as I don't touch them,* I think to myself. She says, "I kind of hate them. I bought them for him for his birthday, and he wouldn't take them when he left. I guess that's what you get for buying someone an animal for their birthday." She shrugs, cueing another empathetic nod from me.

"So how do you want to do this?" I ask tentatively.

"Just make the check out to me. It's month to month, so you can leave with a month's notice. Or I can kick you out."

I laugh nervously and hand her a check for more money than I've ever handed a stranger who didn't work at a bank.

The apartment is precisely decorated, if cramped. I try to think of the dominant colors in her decorating scheme, light blue and brown, as our team colors. The blue and brown towels, carpeting, curtains, living room table are all cheerleading us on as a team! I try to reconsider the owl as our mascot, to make peace with the owl pillows, the owl candlesticks, the small porcelain owl and the stone owl, the owl dishes, the owl potholder. When she reorganizes my groceries and my toiletries, I try to think of her as a spatial savant, rather than OCD. *I can handle this,* I think.

The night that I moved in, Stacey left a key under the doormat for me. She's been away from the apartment for several days. Alone in the apartment, I try to find space for my stuff. No luck — the cupboards and hall closets are all filled to the brim with her things. I leave most of my stuff in boxes until she turns up. Finally, one afternoon she comes home and heads straight for the bath. I'm in my room with my college friend and former Portland roommate, Kristy, who now lives a couple of hours away from me in Sonora.

"This is ridiculous. You get in there and say hello to your new roommate, Cole."

"What? Get in the bath?"

"Once she comes out and goes to her room, count five minutes on your cell phone, and then go knock on her door."

"Ugh."

I gently knock on her door.

"What?"

I seem to have come to call at a bad time, but now there's nothing left to do but soldier on.

"Hi!" I say brightly. "I'm here, and I just wanted to say hi."

"Hold. On," she says firmly, then slowly answers the door.

I wave my hand frantically, more of a drowning, out-to-sea look than a felicitous gesture. Smiling broadly, I look as if I'm about to enter an incredibly gracious seizure.

She is holding a makeup compact and standing in front of a mirror.

"Well, I'm getting ready to go to class."

"Oh, OK. Sorry. We'll talk later then."

I retreat to my room, my heart pounding.

The next night, she apologizes and welcomes me with a big hug. She smells like burning plastic.

July 2009
Tucson, Arizona

Charlie and I are staying at a Motel 6 in the desert. CalArts granted me a stipend for the trip before I graduated, to be recouped in receipts once I return. For now, though, everything has to be paid for up front. This is why we don't have a rental car and we're staying in the cheapest hotel we could find. Tomorrow, our plan is to take the bus together to the ornate hotel hosting the annual Society for Disability Studies conference, where I'm speaking as part of a panel on disability studies and the arts. This is my first academic conference.

Charlie's presence is the insurance I have taken out against myself. He translates the maps for alien bus routes. To me, reading this picture of tangled loops in order to get where I need to go is akin to looking deep into a plate of spaghetti to find my fortune.

He also enters into lengthy negotiations with the motel for towels. I've already been rebuffed twice by housekeeping.

Since we couldn't afford to rent a car after all of my stipend allowance went to lodging and plane tickets, we walk across the motel parking lot in the blazing heat to the closest food source — a Carl's Jr. The Internet at the motel is down, leaving me unable to access my paper, which I had, of course, emailed to myself at the last minute. The night before the conference, we take a couple of buses to the hotel where it will be held.

Each of the conference rooms is named after a different species of cactus. My panel will be in the Agave Room. Charlie walks with me through the hotel to the room where I'm assigned to speak, pointing out visual landmarks — a water fountain, a plaque, the bathrooms — so that I won't get lost on my way to the room where I'm going to present.

"OK, now, do you want to try it yourself?" he asks.

I nod. My independence is won by careful preplanning. I walk the route from the hotel lobby, noting the water fountain, the bathrooms, the plaque for the Agave Room, then walk back.

"OK?"

"OK." I feel brittle, overwhelmed and nervous, but I'm doing my best to keep it to myself.

"Look!" On the walk back to the bus stop, Charlie points out tiny birds living in holes in the cacti. He can tell by my silence that I'm anxious, and he's wisely attempting to divert my anxiety by drawing my attention to tiny, cute animals. But tiny birds cannot save us now. As soon as we get back to the motel, I exhale in a torrent of tears, "This is like living in a fucking Sam Shepard play!" and then retreat to the bathroom, where the floor is cool, still slick in spots with moisture from our showers. He waits, betting correctly that I will feel embarrassed shortly after. I come out of the bathroom to crouch tentatively on the corner of the bed. He sits on a Formica chair by the window. We've kept the shades drawn ever since a van pulled up next door and a man began unloading a series of large plastic vats into the room next door.

"What do you want? Do you want to move to another hotel?"

"No," I sob. "We can't afford the difference."

Neither of us says anything for several minutes until Charlie breaks the silence in his measured, quiet tone. I have to stop sobbing in order to hear him.

"Right now. All. I. Want. To. Do. Is whatever. It. Takes. For you. To stop. Crying."

I pick up my head from my hands and smile, sheepishly.

He has begun scribbling on our receipt from Carl's Jr.

"What are you doing?"

"Hold on."

He continues scribbling, then opens the phone book.

"I am going to get us a rental car."

"A car?"

"A car." He is all business now. "OK, if I'm going to catch the bus to the rental place in time, I have to leave now. I'll use my credit card, and we'll split the cost when we get back."

"Here." Lacking a credit card, I give him all the cash in my wallet. "In case you need to take a cab."

He returns with a red SUV. The next morning, I swallow a handful of herbal antianxiety medication with a swig of bottled water, and we peel out of the parking lot and head for the hotel.

Academic conferences infer expertise, exclusivity, a conferring of like minds.

They're another respite from the body, a meeting about ideas. At the disability studies conference, this difference feels uniquely pressurized.

I'm the last to speak on my panel. My video clips of Orlan, the performance artist I'm speaking about, won't load, and I struggle with the mouse on the unfamiliar computer. I scroll up instead of down, losing my place multiple times as I'm reading my paper aloud. I've almost run out the clock on my allotted time attending to these issues. "Just go on to the slides, then," the moderator says gruffly, but my PowerPoint refuses to load.

During the Q&A, I take a question from a woman in the front row whose skin looks as if it's melting off her face. She's boney with thin blond hair. A pale pink pillbox hat is perched on her head. My first thought is that I wish that I could pull off a hat like that. My next thought is that I can see her tongue and that it reminds me of the dry pebbly tongues of my dad's cockatiels.

"I'm just curious about what you were going to say about Orlan's use of body modification as plastic surgery . . . because I've had several surgeries and each time the surgeons would tell me 'You know, we could change your nose. We could work on your

face.' And I just thought . . . *No thanks.*"
She tightens her lips into a small, wry smile.

I look down at my notes about the French performance artist.

In Orlan's surgery series, her own face became her mask, a highly personal canvas portraying the malleability of identity. However, this is only the first level of her masking. Her greater masking is what draws your attention to her work: the inherent female carnival grotesque involved in plastic surgery as body modification art. Through this mask, Orlan is able to draw your attention to the face and subvert our attachment to physical identity.

What the hell do I know about "subverting our attachment to physical identity" that the woman in front of me doesn't know already? My head swimming, I look up at her and back down at my notes.

My mask is not just in the hiding of my disability; it is also inherent in how I choose to reveal it. My body, my head, is a physical container for my brain — the site of my neurological disability. It is also a mask of normality, carrying in my physicality the outward assurance that I am just like everyone else. This is only one mask that I wear. The other I put on when I choose to reveal my condition in writing. In articulating my difference, I make textual choices in tone, style, and construct that reveal as they hide.

Nothing, there is nothing here that I can tell her. I nod and smile and say, "Well . . . it was about the face and the soul, and if, if we change our faces, do we change, do we change who we are? *But* that's obviously a very essentialist —"

The moderator interrupts me. "OK, so a feminist rescue read of Orlan. Great. That's all the time we have."

Charlie drives the SUV back to the Motel 6, where we eat chocolate chip ice cream out of the container with a shared plastic spoon, unwrap the plastic cups from their sanitizing cellophane sheaths, fill them with whiskey, and toast to my inaugural academic flame-out.

When Charlie and I open the door to my apartment back in Oakland, Stacey is standing in the middle of the kitchen in a T-shirt and her panties, cutting the hair of some skinny tattooed guy who's sitting on a stool. She has a giant scrape on her chin, which she scratches at before taking the guy's hair between her fingers to measure her next cut.

"Hey, how's it going?" The guy smiles at me, clearly pleased with the situation.

I muster a cold "Hey" and head to my room to place my bags on my bed and take a moment to myself to assess what I've witnessed. Charlie follows me quietly to my room and then, sensing that I could use some breathing space, cracks open the door just as my pantsless roommate is exiting the bathroom.

"Hey — what happened to your face?" he says, with a look of concern.

"Oh, I fell. Isn't it *sexy*?" She strikes a model pose.

Never great with sarcasm, he responds plainly, "No. It looks upsetting."

I suggest to Charlie that we go grab lunch at an Indian restaurant down the street.

On the way, I try to explain, calmly, "It's never a good idea to call a woman's face upsetting. Even if she has a bruise. It doesn't make her feel good about it."

"Oh, OK." He pauses to think this over. "I agree. Well. What should I have said instead?"

"How about: 'That looks painful, I'm sorry that happened to you'?"

"Oh. Right. OK."

The next morning, Charlie drives back from Oakland to Santa Barbara. Charlie and I have made this trip together many times. The last time that we did it, we stopped in Sacramento and spent the night at his mom's house.

"She's doing so much better. She has a job and her own place and it's . . . A few years ago it would have been impossible to stay with her. Out of the question. You don't understand what a big deal this is, that it's actually clean enough for us to stay there." He was looking at the road before us, but I could hear in his voice that he was tearing up.

Minerva was meeting us there the next day, but that night, it was just us. Charlie's mom was a square-shaped woman who smiled a lot. Her apartment was dark but clean. Before we got into the car to pick up Minerva from the train station, she said, "Wait, hold on, I need your help cleaning out the car."

"Mom, we're taking my car."

"I know, I know, I just . . . while you're here."

She handed each of us a garbage bag and took one herself. We headed to the parking lot. It was obvious which car was hers.

When Charlie and I got into his car, after

cleaning out his mom's car, I said nothing. I acted as if it had never happened. I didn't know what to say. We were both silent for most of the drive. Finally, he said quietly, "She really is doing so much better."

I put my hand on his thigh. "I know."

A few days after Charlie left, I'm in the small living room area of the Oakland apartment checking my email and drinking coffee around ten in the morning when Stacey walks in. We exchange morning acknowledgments as she's dialing a number into her phone and then begins speaking sharply to whoever picked up.

"Hey. Thank you. No, I don't have any plans. I was supposed to have lunch with my sister, but she bailed on me. No. I don't want it to be my birthday. Oh, OK, fine. Maybe we'll meet up later."

She hangs up the phone.

"Happy un-birthday," I say warmly, trying to make a joke.

"Thanks," she says.

"Do you have any plans?"

"No. Well, tomorrow night I'm renting out a bar. But I don't have any plans tonight."

She comes home at 3:00 a.m., opens the door to my bedroom to wake me up. "Daaaaaarling, daaaaaarling . . . can I have some whiskey? It's my birthday!"

"Happy birthday."

I press the half-empty bottle of whiskey left over from Charlie's last visit in her hands and close the door to my room. She heads to her room with a guy and blasts heavy metal.

The next morning, I see her as I'm walking up the street. Her little Yorkie puppy runs toward me, looking like a little burrito with bangs. When I practiced the following words in my head, they somehow sounded like the perfect act of self-assertion, with a dash of wry humor to deflect anger. "Hey, so I know it was your birthday last night, but in the future, maybe not power ballads at five-thirty in the morning?" I smile nervously. Yeah. Great. Way to go, me. Her silence confirms my dread, but it's too late; I must press on.

"So, are we good?"

She says nothing.

"OK?"

She nods.

"OK." I bend down to pet her little burrito. "See you in a bit."

I head into the apartment, make myself a peanut butter and jelly sandwich, and sit down at the dining room table. This moment is crucial; I must appear relaxed and chat about little things to defuse the tension of our confrontation and to show her that I harbor no resentment toward her and the moment is fully behind us. She enters with the dog, both of them skittering into the kitchen.

"So," I begin tentatively, "I hear that they want to make a speak-easy out of the basement?" Nice, building chatter, safe ground. She stiffens.

"I haven't heard anything about that. And even if it were true, I doubt that anyone would tell me because I'm technically the building manager. Look. So now I can't have a party in my own room? On my birthday? I can't have a party in my own room on my birthday." She's boxed herself into a little pouty blond rectangle of limbs on the couch, her arms crossed over her legs, which are pressed against her chest.

What I should have said in response: "No, of course you can do whatever you like in your room. You can fete yourself into a coma just because it's Wednesday — a nice, quiet coma. I really don't care as long as you don't wake me up."

What she said: "I just don't know why you're always in your room and you never sit and watch TV with me. It's just so weird, you're just, I don't know, you're just being so weird. You're not acting comfortable. I'm just not sure that this is going to work."

I am being thrown out for not being comfortable. This does little to ease my comfort level.

"You have your own silverware," she continues. "Who has their own silverware? Why don't you just use mine?"

"I owned silverware before I lived here, and I brought it with me?"

I'm furrowing my brow and waiting for a break in her tirade of my offenses when her cell phone breaks out into Joy Division's "Love Will Tear Us Apart." She pounces on it.

"Yeah? OK, you want to get some food or something? No, hey, meet me at the BART station on Twelfth, and we'll get some food."

I just sit there and wait for her to finish her call so that we can resume arguing.

"I don't know, we'll figure it out when we get there. Just meet me there, and we'll figure it out. Look, I've got someone on the other line; just meet me there, and we'll figure it out."

She switches over to the other line.

"Hello? Oh, I'm OK." She shoots me an accusatory look. "Hold on."

She switches over again.

"BART! Twelfth Street!" She mumbles,

"He's still on drugs," and switches back.

"Can I call you in like an hour?" Again with the look in my direction. "OK. Great." Click.

I grab hold of the pause in conversation to begin my defense.

"Look, we obviously didn't get off on the best foot," I say. "When I first introduced myself, it was obviously not the best time —"

"I just got out of the shower! Obviously! Who does that? Who trails someone *out of the shower*?"

But I had waited! I had intentionally waited! I don't want to derail the conversation by defending myself to her. At this point, however, I'm no longer sure what the point is or what my intended outcome was. Am I fighting to stay here? Am I throwing down the gauntlet and moving out? Am I being thrown out? Can she even do that?

While I was trying to quickly consider my strategy, she had continued her rant, and now I'm confused. Goddamn it — I'm toast. But, what's this? She seems to have meandered into a personal anecdote.

"I just got out of rehab," she tells me, "and my boyfriend broke up with me, and then I got mugged . . ."

"Wow. I'm really sorry that all of that happened to you; is there anything I can do to help?" I sound like an empathetically programmed robot.

"I just don't want there to be any *animosity* between us!" she screams.

When I stare at her blankly, she slaps both hands on the collaged coffee table for emphasis; this apparently signals the endgame because she stands up as if something has been settled.

"OK, so, no hard feelings, bitches," she says.

Then she juts her fist out, as if to punch me. I wrap my arms around her; she is so much smaller than me. This is self-defense disguised as affection.

"Um," she says. "I was trying to bump you. Like, fist-bump you?"

She then gestures toward her phone, which is silent for now.

"He's a famous graffiti artist. Flake."

"Huh?"

"That's what he goes by; his handle is Flake."

"Oh yeah, I know Flake."

Flake is best known for tagging album covers of 1980s hair-metal bands with his handle, in bright neon bubble letters.

"Yeah, everyone always says, I mean, said, 'Ohmygod, your boyfriend's *Flake*?' " She shakes her head in a mixture of mockery and evident pride.

I obviously need to get the hell out of here. Charlie's not ready for me to move in with him in Santa Barbara. He's started making noises about wanting to see other people "but not break up. I'd still come to the Bay Area once a month." I am too afraid to address his proposal directly, and eventually he stops bringing it up. At this point, we've continued to date through a variety of geographic inconveniences, but although the physical distance is less than it was when he lived in Seattle and I was in school in Valencia, the difference between his busy grad student life and my lonely unemployed one is a wider chasm than the literal distance. I'm not sure where this leaves us. With no job in sight and a relationship at loose ends, I see no other choice but to move back to the same city as my parents.

Ditzy.

Definition: impulsive, silly.

Synonyms: bemused, brainless, bubble-headed, capricious, careless, changeable, changeful, dizzy, empty-headed, erratic, fickle, flighty, flustered, frivolous, gaga, heedless, inconstant, irresolute, irresponsible, light-headed, punchy, reckless, reeling, scatterbrained, skittish, slaphappy, thoughtless, unbalanced, unsettled, unstable, unsteady, vacillating, volatile, whimsical, whirling, wild, woozy.

Antonyms: calm, careful, level-headed, sensible, serious.

I am a young woman. That's why I bring my mother with me when I sign my rental agreement for my new apartment in Portland and consult her about the math. This is my first studio apartment, my first attempt at living independently. The representative from the rental company arrives in a dark suit and opens the door with a flourish. He is about my age, and once I tell him I am on Social Security, he stops making eye contact with me and speaks mainly to my mother. The apartment broker and I have entered into a silent understanding that is still new to me. He cannot ask why I, a perfectly healthy and able-bodied twenty-eight-year-old, am on Social Security. In exchange for my privacy, he can assume whatever he wants. This is the latest calculation I've learned to make — bargaining for my privacy with my dignity. I just wish he would return to looking me in the eyes when he speaks to me. Still, I'm very lucky; being a young woman is a wonderful disguise. Being a young man would have been a much worse disguise. Men are expected to know and to lead; there's less cultural space for men to just be ditzy. I would have had a much harder time hiding out as a man.

A week after I move in, Charlie and I have a fight on the phone about how I failed to call him back when he called to say that his aunt was ill. He breaks up with me; I send daisies to his cottage in Santa Barbara. The note attached is a quote from one of our favorite movies, *The Big Lebowski.* "Nothing is fucked here, Dude." It's not quite as true as we'd both like it to be, but the gesture acts as a tourniquet, not healing everything but stopping the relationship from bleeding out until we can tend to it properly together in person. He calls me to say, "I like what we've built, what we've built together. I'll come to Portland in a couple of weeks, I'll see your new place, and we'll work this all out."

I'm naked in his arms in my new bed when he says to the ceiling, "My therapist said that I shouldn't bring this up unless I'm serious. I've been attracted to other people, and that's something I'd like to explore. But I don't want us to break up."

"We've been through this. If you want to see other people I get that, but I don't think that I could be one of those people." He says nothing for a long time. My mind starts to race.

"Is there . . . someone specific?"

He opens his mouth to speak, shuts it again, opens and shuts it again, then finally and unconvincingly settles on "No."

I wordlessly get out of bed and into the bathroom, closing the door with an embarrassing amount of force. This was a new twist on the same old argument. I take some deep breaths, splash water on my face, and walk back out. He's made a nest for himself out of blankets in the corner where the bed meets the wall.

"I've changed my mind. That was inappropriate. I mean not inappropriate. I should say what I feel. I want you. I want to do this. Not . . . that."

We go round and round like this all weekend. In the pit of my stomach I know that I have to be the one to put an end to it, but I don't know how to. I feel as if I have nothing left without him. Without a job, school, friends, a boyfriend, I don't know how to build my identity on my own. Again, I'm learning how to become who I already am.

In my first semester of grad school I took a class called Autobiography, for which I read a book called *Sylvia*, about a turbulent relationship set in Greenwich Village in the 1960s. The professor referred to the book as "an example of heterosexual bathos." I asked my dad what she meant by this phrase. He cackled, "I don't think you heard her right. I think she must have meant *pathos*. Heterosexual *pathos*. But bathos, pathos, what's the difference?" *Pathos* is a sentiment of compassion or pity; *bathos* is an anticlimax, a sense of disillusionment.

Through these circular fights with Charlie, I was learning the difference.

Living in this town is like living beneath a mossy rock. It's moist and dark and a good place to grow drugs or write a book. Kick over the rock, and you find a population of almost six hundred thousand people, loping away from the light. Many will be plugged into headphones; a surprising number will be clutching a cigarette between their lips; some will be holding a paper cup of coffee. If you're in the southern part of the city, many people will be white. If you are in the north, many people will be black (although this is becoming less true as the tendrils of gentrification creep up Mississippi Avenue). The north is already unrecognizable from when I lived in the key lime green house a couple of years ago. Back then the closest restaurant was a strip club with paint peeling off the walls, and our house was broken into regularly; when we called the cops or the local pawn shops to try to track down our stuff, we were met with amused disinterest. Now there's a strip of stores with cruelty-free clothing and a sushi place.

If you're in downtown Portland from nine to five, a variety of races will be wearing suits or blazers or barista smocks. After five (it gets dark at 4:30 p.m. in the winter), a ghost army will be pushing shopping carts containing their life's possessions through the streets. Portland has a fairly large homeless population given how difficult it is to find a dry bench. Portland is nowhere anyone goes looking for trouble. It's a place where trouble grows slowly, in dark crevices, if you stay still for too long.

There is no hard alcohol on grocery store shelves in Oregon, a fact that I alternately curse and raise up as my salvation. In 1846, William Johnson, the former "high sheriff" of Portland, was indicted for the "retailing of ardent spirits." According to the indictment, Johnson, "being moved or reduced by an evil heart, did sell, barter, give or trade ardent spirits." Though I haven't been able to prove it, I like to think that my street, Northwest Johnson Street, around the corner from several bars, is named for this man.

Portland is home to a variety of migratory tribes, the most well known being the twentysomethings who drift into and out of town. It's late April when I move back, and the swifts, tiny sparrows that make up Portland's other migratory flock, are swooping in and out of the chimney of the elementary school by my apartment. The dark swarms remind me of video I've seen of the bats living under the Congress Avenue Bridge in Austin, Texas, another home to migratory twentysomethings.

I refer to my new upstairs neighbor, whom I've yet to encounter in person, as Hooker Boots. When she isn't clomping around upstairs in what sound like leaden stilettos, she's hammering away at building what can only be some sort of depraved Rube Goldberg device. Her other hobby is to loudly practice her gymnastic exploits. I can see her now, in her patent leather tool belt and little else, like the beginning of a bad porno. "All of this hammering just makes me *so horny . . .*"

Parallel play, a developmental psychology term used to describe two- to three-year-olds who play side-by-side with other children without interaction, perfectly describes my Portland life. Because my parents moved here when I was already out of school and I've shifted living in and out of town, I don't know anyone here very well, and every time I come back I'm of course older and it feels harder to meet people than the last time I was here.

My friend Allison suggests that we meet at the Burnside Skatepark, the concrete bowl under the Burnside Bridge. Neither of us is a skateboarder, but she told me that she comes down to watch the regulars skate whenever she's feeling down and finds that it helps.

We stand to the side of the park and watch the skaters, mostly men in their early twenties and late thirties and a couple of women, swoop and occasionally tumble. Allison tells me about her friend Grant, who lives in one of the industrial-looking brick apartment buildings overlooking the park and comes to watch the skaters with her sometimes, comparing watching the skaters to watching the migration of the swallows of Capistrano. Grant is in a wheelchair, due to a degenerative disease.

I have been thinking a lot about home, how for some people it is a fixed point, a North Star in the astrology making up their personal narrative. For others, like me, it's a destination that I chart and rechart, less any brick-and-mortar place than a sensation that I chase after and then find or misplace or let go of and then chase again.

I meet up with my friend Delores after her shift at Vowel. Delores was my next-door neighbor when I first moved to Portland. We catch up about the graphic design work she's been doing more seriously lately, about her boyfriend whom she now lives with. She's been helping him learn to cope with his mental illness, which has begun to shake her faith. "The only thing that would make me not believe in God is schizophrenia. To have no control over your own mind. How could you do that to someone?"

Schizophrenics use stories to make sense of feeling paranoid, will internalize narratives to explain to themselves the overwhelmingly inexplicable. We all crave context. I've become increasingly obsessed with narration, story, how we organize and contain an overwhelming life.

Writing about my world feels both like willing my truest self into being while inevitably obliterating that same self. Writing is the connective network between my body and my brain; it tells my body what to do. It's also a preemptive defensive strike. The only way that I know to try to keep my poise is through my vulnerability, but in the process of explaining I risk losing that which I'm striving to keep. I write to connect with a disorienting and sometimes indifferent universe.

On bad days, I'm too overwhelmed by navigating the outside world to leave my apartment, which I refer to as the Fortress of Ineptitude. I read, I clean, I write, I mess around on the Internet, I test out new recipes.

On these rough days, I think about how it will happen: I will not see the car coming around the corner, from my left side. I'll be lost in my own thoughts, and then, suddenly, the air will be knocked out of me. I am tumbling over the hood, thinking, *Well, here it is,* or maybe if I'm having a really bad day I will think, *Finally.* In my head I am always frozen midtumble, over the roof of the car like a detective chasing down a perp in the opening credits to some cop show from the 1970s.

It won't be a surprise. Crossing the street, I often think, *Well, this could go one of two ways.* One day I will miscalculate how far, how fast, enough time, not enough time, and the car won't have time to screech to a halt and lay on the horn like the other times. The driver won't have time to be angry, and, ideally, I won't have time to be scared.

This is how it will happen: I will fall off the map. I will get lost again in the wrong neighborhood at the wrong time. I am panicked but determined to get back on track. I run a groove in the pavement with my sneakers. My cell phone runs out of batteries. I stop at newsstands, where I attempt to translate wild pointing; I grip maps written on scraps of newsprint or cocktail napkins, follow the cul-de-sac of a stranger's handwriting down an alley and then across a bridge. I will sleep on a bench and then in a storefront when it rains. Undeterred, I will continue my quest. Eventually, concrete gives way to earth, the city to the countryside, and as I cross fields of corn and cabbage and disentangle myself from archaic, winding sprinkler systems, I begin to lose my mind. I solicit scarecrows, sleep in henhouses, until one morning I bleed into the horizon.

This is how it will happen: Slowly, gradually, they will erode me — kerfuffles, little misunderstandings, raised eyebrows. These are the little microbes of embarrassment that infect my dignity, the germs that attack and invade my sense of self. They ride in on the Trojan horse of other people's harmless assumptions and the pressure that I put on myself, as if when I miscalculate change or don't understand my own bills I am breaking an unspoken code about what it means to be an adult.

The most immediate form of relief is to put on an album, close my eyes, and allow my body to melt into nowhere and no one. With my eyes closed and the right album, I can sneak out of the rind of my body to become shapeless pulp.

There's a big brick hospital a few blocks down from my new studio apartment. On one especially rotten day, unemployed and watching my long-distance relationship crumble like a bad movie starring someone else, I realize that I could just walk into the hospital and ask for a stay in the psych ward. Nobody could stop me; I wouldn't need a ride there, unlike other times when I begged my parents to take me. It's still tempting to shake the temptation to walk into a hospital and say, "Hey, I'm exhausted. Why don't you take the wheel for a while?" I still want to believe in the authority of a hospital to heal me. I'm still afraid that I don't have the tools myself.

It's still difficult for me to shake the notion that anyone can walk into a hospital with enough urgency and be righted. Back here in Portland I am only starting to understand that learning how to be good to yourself *for* yourself is a painstakingly gradual one. It is a process that I don't yet have the patience or compassion for. I just want to be loved.

On good days, I am a goddamn mutant superhero. On good days, your planet, with its dependence on maps and clocks, is inferior to the homeland of my interior world. On good days, I maneuver the terrain of your world bemused by your customs.

"You know, you don't have to use that word — *disabled*." My new Portland therapist frowns. She looks vaguely like my mom, but she's much meaner. I told her early on to give it to me straight; I can take it, I said. I've been on the proverbial couch since middle school — give me your best shot. "I know a man, whatshisname, he ran for office here . . . Roy! Oh, Roy, well, Roy has one hand, he lost the other in an accident, and he says, 'I'm not disabled. Fuck disabled.' He has an artificial hand. He can do pretty much whatever he wants."

It's important to me that the word *disabled* validates, in a very physical manner, my previously nebulous cloud of internal neurological symptoms. It is a very stable word; an assertive, clear word for *cannot*. As someone with an invisible disability, I use this uncomfortable word in part because it's difficult. *Disabled* says yes, this is real. It says you cannot see it, but it is here and it can see you. Identifying as disabled also means that I carry all of the connotations of the word, none of them positive: helpless, damaged, et cetera.

I'm looking for a word that doesn't exist yet. I'm looking for a word that unifies as it implies exclusivity. Having spent most of my adolescent and young adult life studiously, preciously, avoiding labels, I find myself in my late twenties on the hunt for one.

I have a word for the kind of person who I am not — *neurotypical* — which would imply that I have a word for the kind of person who I am — *neurodiverse* — but while it's incredibly broad (encompassing, as the term implies, anyone and everyone whose brain functions differently from the norm), it's also overtly clinical. Whether the word is coined, like *neurodiverse,* or is a more charged word reclaimed from its negative connotation (like *crip* or *mad*), words about disability are used to compartmentalize more than unify.

I want a word that is a home address. I am looking for a name that pushes the role of language about disability outside of the binary of *can* versus *can't.* How do I find a word that simultaneously communicates strength and weakness? A word that recognizes that they are not parallel traits but instead shaped more like a double helix? Ability and inability are two hands belonging to one person, each shaking the other. I read in my phenomenology class that when you shake one hand with your other hand, it's impossible to feel each hand individually clasping the other. You can see it, so you know it must be true, but you cannot feel the press of one palm independent from the press of your other palm. I am looking for a word for my body that articulates the intractable, invisible link between my weakness and my strength. I want to make it linguistically impossible for me to feel one without feeling the other.

■ ■ ■ ■

V.
RETURN

■ ■ ■ ■

"I could tell you my adventures — beginning from this morning," said Alice a little timidly: "but it's no use going back to yesterday, because I was a different person then."
— Lewis Carroll, *Alice in Wonderland*

March 2010
Portland, Oregon/Saratoga, New York

It's 2:00 a.m. in the Portland airport. I'm about to board the plane to New York to meet my uncle, who will drive me to my first writing residency, in the woods of upstate New York.

I've applied to two PhD programs in writing since graduating from CalArts, three months shy of a year ago, but despite my most concentrated efforts I somehow managed to misfile the copies of my applications for both. I will have to wait out the year if I plan to apply again, and, left to my own devices, what's to stop me from making the same mistakes again? It's an honest-to-God mystery to me what I did, where I slipped up with the paperwork this time. I'm exasperated with myself. I had this same issue with organizing my college and MFA applications, and I struggle with job applica-

263

tions as well. I am the empress of clerical error.

This is the first and only writing residency that I've applied to. When I asked a visiting professor for advice on what to do once I graduate from CalArts, he said, "Just live in your car and go to writing residencies. That's what I did." So I applied to one that I'd heard authors I admire refer to in interviews and acknowledgments, one where you get a studio to write in and they cook your meals, just to take a shot in the dark. Someone dropped out at the last minute, leaving a six-week window free, which I nabbed as soon as it was offered to me.

While waiting to board, I notice an attractive young man stretched out in a bank of chairs by himself. He's wearing a thick gray sweater and clutching a guitar case, with the kind of artfully disheveled hair that wouldn't be out of place in either Portland or Brooklyn, since they're on the way to becoming the same town. I wonder vaguely if he's some famous or semi-famous musician, heading from one show to another. I'm behind him in line as we board, and he turns his head to smile knowingly at me as he puts his baggage up in the overhead compartment above his seat. I can't decide if I dislike him for looking smug, or if I'm attracted to him, or both. I'm in the row ahead of him, and as we take off I can hear him describing the sound of the Indian drum, the tabla, to his neighbor. "It's just beautiful. Like running water." The plane is more than half empty; for the length of the flight most of us sleep cradled in our own rows in the dark of the unlit cabin. I feel as if the three hours I'm losing to another time zone are being physically leached from my body as I shift and squirm over my empty three-chair row and try unsuccessfully to fall asleep.

Close to the end of the flight, the plane's deicer breaks down and we're rerouted to Buffalo for several hours, unable to land in New York City. Once we deplane, I immediately turn the corner to plug my dead cell phone into a socket to charge under a wide window. I sit down in a bank of chairs next to the window, to watch planes take off and land. Then I decide that I need coffee first, unplug my cell phone, and wheel my carry-on luggage over to a coffee cart. When I return, my imaginary famous musician is in the row of chairs watching the planes take off, a book in his lap. I don't want to have to think about deciding whether or not to speak to him. Instead, I talk to my mom on my plugged-in cell phone and try to sneak furtive peeks at what he's reading, but I can't see the cover of his book. I'm afraid to take any risks, to open a door to even a slight possibility. I'm a rabid guard dog protecting what Charlie and I have. Having just flown two thousand miles away from him, I'm afraid of wandering any farther by getting lost even a little bit in a conversation with a stranger. I'm afraid that right now any move that I make in a new direction will make it more difficult for me to find my way back home to him. Sometimes when I'm lost, the only thing I know to do is to stand still.

I notice that the young man is wearing an expensive brand of shoes that my dad loves and always buys on sale at discount department stores. "They're worn by the king of Spain!" my dad says, trying to persuade me to wear them. "So ugly, but soooo comfortable." *Talk to him about his shoes,* a little voice in my head says, but then I think that sounds too transparent, so I say nothing. On the flight from Buffalo to JFK, I finally fall asleep and dream that I'm climbing a ladder with rungs of broken discolored piano keys.

I spend a couple of days at my uncle Ron and aunt Linda's apartment in Brooklyn with my two younger cousins before Ron drives me out into the woods. The night that I arrive at the residency I stand under a large maple tree in the dark with my cell phone, in mock privacy, to call Charlie. After several rings he picks up, sounding out of breath.

"Hey!" I wait for him to catch his breath.

He answers, speaking very slowly. "Heeeey . . . How's it *goooing*?"

"You sound . . . weird."

"I'm biking. To a party. I'm. Out of breath."

"Oh. Cool. Whose party?"

He's silent for a long time.

"I'm biking to the party of the woman who I am attracted to," he says with a flat, even tone. I wish that there was a map to lead me either out of this relationship or more deeply into it.

I blurt out, "Fuck it."

I want to slam my phone against the tree.

"I can't. I can't do this now. You know who you are, Charlie? You're just like Ducky."

"Danny's *parakeet*?"

"It's like, it's like I put out my finger for you to hop onto it and you, you bite me. So I keep my finger out because biting is how a bird tests for sturdiness in a branch, and I try to keep it still and you *bite me again and*

267

again. I'm getting afraid to put my finger out."

Now I'm running out of breath.

"Charlie. I need you to just hop on."

"I've never been in a relationship that I haven't felt ambivalent about."

"It's been *years.* I'm not . . . I'm not some exotic mystery girl."

"But you kind of are. I've never met anyone from outer space before."

One of the artists has started a meditation group at the residency. Every evening at 5:45, we meet in the living room of one of the cottages that make up the tiny village of the residency. I sit on the rug with my legs crossed next to several other artists, three feet from a couch on which, according to local legend, Sylvia Plath and Ted Hughes once had sex. In this spot, I try to desire nothing.

I'm trying to learn how to meditate, to just sit here and not hope for anything. The Zen books that the other artists lend me say that once I give up hope, I will enter the palace of nothingness and nothing will be better or worse — everything will be just as it is, and it will be neither horrible or wonderful, it will just be in between — and that is the grand prize that is not a prize. I am trying to fit everything I am onto the splinter of this very second, but my feelings keep spilling over like a water cracker overloaded with expensive-smelling cheese at some cocktail party you didn't really want to attend until the cracker breaks and then you're walking around with a crumpled napkin, smiling and chatting with guests when all you can think about is where the trash can is hidden. I'm trying to tenderly, gently not care about anything. I'm trying so hard to not give a fuck in the most compassionate way possible. Of course, just by trying I'm already totally screwed.

At one of the nightly dinners toward the end of my six-week stay, I motion to the trees outside the window that are doubled over, as if by lightning. "I wonder what's up with those." A performance artist tells me that the cabbie who drove him into town also pointed out the trees. "They all split in two here, even all the old ones. You know why? It rains so much here in the summer that the trees don't need to grow roots deep into the earth. All of their roots are shallow, on the surface. They are not rooted deeply to the earth, so eventually they topple, broken in two by their own weight."

The performance artist looks at me, widening his eyes. "I mean, it's just so . . .

evocative."

The next morning when I'm doing my laundry, I drop a pair of graying granny panties out of the dryer in front of the editor of a national fashion magazine. Everyone here is smarter and fancier than me. I'm barely out of my MFA program; I bungled my PhD applications; even my boyfriend isn't feeling especially fond of me right now. I'm a bundle of nerves most of the time at the residency, and I feel like a total imposter being here, I'm so in awe of this world.

In the evenings after dinner we often walk over to the carriage house to play a billiards game in which you don't use pool cues; you just run around the table and try to use one billiard ball to hit another one across the table and into a pocket. Of course I'm terrible at this game, but it's the most fun that I have at the residency. I'm the worst at it, but I play often; I'm trying to teach myself that participating is more important than the quality of my participation. One night after I lose another game, a painter comes up to me and says, "I don't understand. You keep getting yourself out in ways that don't even make sense."

I think of Denis, my old math tutor, saying to me from across the folding table in his living room, "I could help you if you got the problem wrong the same way every time, but you do it differently each time."

I don't know if I want to go home, or if I want to be as far from home as possible. I don't even know where home would be. Can I be both at home and far from it, here? Staying put, just sitting with my feelings in those meditations, feels a whole lot like running screaming with my hair on fire. Meditation, with its focus on the present, makes narration impossible. It is a respite from the story I tell myself of who I am and why. It is an oasis on a map. As with an oasis, I am never sure if the peace that meditation promises is nearly within my grasp or just a shimmering mirage.

My only way in to the evening meditation sessions is to breathe in confusion, pain, and frustration. I breathe out relief. Breathe out relief not just for yourself, but for everyone feeling what you are feeling right now, one of my books says. So I breathe out relief for Kristy, who is self-harming again. I breathe in and imagine her in the bathroom of the tiny nonprofit she works for in Northern California, locking the bathroom door and biting her arms just to feel something, and I breathe out. I'm greedy for relief for myself, so I'm quick to send it on my breath for others.

Many of my old college friends are now scattered around the globe, trying on new homes and careers. Miranda is working at an acupuncture resort in Thailand; Peter is in the Middle East working for a nonprofit. I'm a few months shy of thirty, and it feels as if every week a new news article pops up asking why people of my generation are so late to find a job, get married, settle down. It's as if we've all wandered off somewhere on a school trip, and previous generations are herding us back into two lines with our partners.

Kristy wears a little silver medallion around her neck of Saint Jude, the patron saint of lost causes. She bought it at the gift shop at the Grotto, a Catholic nunnery, when we were living together in Portland after graduating from Johnston. When she was thirteen, Kristy did a stint in what she refers to as the loony bin.

If Saint Jude answers your prayers, you're supposed to put a brief notice in the personals section thanking him. "Thank you to Saint Jude for answering my prayers" will usually suffice. Now that I've nearly survived my twenties, all of my writing at the residency feels like a thank-you to Saint Jude.

August 2010
Santa Barbara, California

On the way back from the residency, I stop in Santa Barbara for a week before heading back to Portland. One night, Charlie takes a frozen pizza out of the oven, places it on the counter, and says, "I think you should move in with me. The problem is distance; the problem is just that you're not here enough, and I'm not there enough."

I want to believe so hard in a problem outside of the two of us, like other people or distance, that I'm more than willing to agree. I feel as if I'm failing at everything; I can't afford to fail at this too right now. I lived by myself in Portland for a total of four months, the first time I ever lived independently, although living in the same town as my parents is still not that independent and neither is moving in with Charlie, but I've never lived with a

273

significant other before so it *feels* like some sort of vague progress toward adulthood.

The night we move all of my belongings out of my studio and into a rental minivan, it's pouring rain. We spend the night in an environmentally conscious motel in Danville, California, called Gaia, the same motel I stayed in with my parents when they moved me out of downtown Oakland back to Portland in their minivan. I chose this place because I remember that it has a small pond with swans, and I had romantic visions of watching the swans with Charlie. But because I don't drive, he has to drive the entire way, and we're only halfway through, and already he's exhausted and his back aches, and I feel guilty. The noise of a wedding in the banquet hall near the pond is scaring the swans tonight. They paddle skittishly around the perimeter of the small artificial lake. We stand on the little wooden bridge over the pool and watch the braver swans bathe themselves in the sprinkling fountain in the center, then we go to sleep. The next day we notice that the minivan has begun to smell like fish. Mysteriously, the source seems to be my 1950s tulip-shaped lamp.

The sky in Santa Barbara is that deep blue of the ocean in TV commercials for

Caribbean resorts. It makes sense to me that I've now landed in a transitional town, where a large chunk of the population are either students or tourists. I'm neither; my tag here is "trailer," which is how grad students and faculty on campus refer nonchalantly to the partner who's just along for the ride.

It's nearly impossible to afford living here, although more and more it seems nearly impossible to afford to live anywhere. Those who can afford to live here full time live a sort of parallel existence to the students at the university, who live parallel to the locals in service jobs at bars, restaurants, hotels, or chain stores in the mall. We live in the same small town, but we shop at different stores, favor different beaches and bars. The Mexican laborers live a parallel existence that I know even less of. All that I know of the family next door to our place, with three young boys who play soccer in the street behind our houses, is that they have a shiny new red truck and a collection of crushed beer and soda cans overspilling in several trash bags in the backyard, where the mother pins up the laundry to dry.

When people from Charlie's department, where he's at least four years away from finishing his PhD, mostly men in their late twenties or early thirties, or their significant others ask me what I do for a living, I tell them that I teach English online. This is partially true; I do teach intro-to-essay classes online sometimes. I don't know how to tell other people that the majority of my income comes from Social Security. I've made some offhanded comments about not being able to drive, explaining that I have a hard time telling how far apart the cars are or how fast they are going, and usually leave it at that. No one really notices or cares; most of my interactions here are made up of the same polite introductory small talk repeated over and over again before the students delve into departmental gossip and talking about computer codes.

Most of our friends here are newly married couples. I never really thought that deeply about marriage in my twenties until right after college, when three of my old friends from high school whom I'd been out of touch with all got married and divorced within the span of the same year. I congratulated myself on not getting married young, but it was really just a matter of circumstance that kept our roles from being reversed, one of those circumstances being that I'm terrified and they took a risk, were vulnerable and committed in a way that I wasn't sure that I could be. Now I suddenly feel as if I have to take a firm position on marriage one way or the other, especially because I'm signing petitions and voting to extend the right to marriage to everyone.

Once, when I was right out of college, just beginning the latest rounds of anti-depressants and therapists, I met for an initial and final therapy session with a blond woman in her late forties with a thick headband. She had two large photos in the room of her sons in their military school outfits. "What do you want to be?" she asked me, and I spat out, "I want to be Patti Smith in the seventies." She glared at me coldly and took her time replying. "You, my dear, are no hothouse flower."

Invisibility is a poisonous privilege. I feel as if I'm constantly withholding, and at the same time I don't know how to explain, where to begin, how many times I'm going to have to repeat the story of my brain to people I barely know. This information that I lived a quarter of my life not knowing myself now feels essential for others to really know me. The other option is to let people assume untrue things about my character: that I am ditzy, not paying attention, silly, stupid. Maybe I'm not yet ready to let go of assuming these things myself. I want to be normal, and I want to be different. It's always been a gradient scale. Everyone has secret truths, circumstantial, biological, historical; everyone weighs what they are willing to risk in trying to connect with another human.

One afternoon while folding laundry together before Charlie leaves for campus, I instigate a fight. When he leaves for campus he often doesn't come back until late at night, and I don't want him to leave me alone again.

"I feel like you're pushing me away with your work," I say to him as I'm folding towels in the bathroom.

"Well, I'm really into my work. And I need to be at school to do my work. So yes, then I am pushing you away with my work."

Almost as soon as I moved in, he began spending more and more time on campus, at band practice, at the bar, anywhere but at the cottage that we share. I feel guilty because I know that he grew up taking care of his mother; I don't want him to feel as if now he has to take care of me.

His avoidance and my feelings of being misunderstood trigger some of my old "crisis behavior," pushing him even further away. When he won't see me or speak to me for days, I feel as if I'm being boiled alive, and the urgency of this feeling extinguishes my ability to speak. Instead I throw my suitcase down the stairs, accidentally (I think) smashing a glass door at the bottom. Screaming for someone to love you is just as self-defeating as screaming for quiet.

Afterward I don't remember much other than feeling exhausted, as if a virus had racked my body. Charlie was left feeling terrified and powerless. When I told him how guilty and ashamed I felt, he chalked it up to "our wicked dynamic." The more that I need him, the more he needs to escape me, and vice versa until all of our interactions become cyclical.

Feeling hopeless, I answer a Craigslist ad to see a room in a house a couple of miles away mainly to prove to myself that I can even as my heart is in my stomach. On the way to the house, I get lost and end up unintentionally circling back to our back door.

I sign us up for couples therapy, where I remain loyal to a fault to the narrative I tell myself of who we are, grad student and girlfriend temporarily displaced in a resort town. Our fights don't fit in the story of us. The more that I try to edit them out, the more the recut jerks and bucks against the frame.

"You lose yourself in relationships," the couples therapist says to me. "You lose your sense of self." She says "you're bright," and it feels like a counterweight to something dark inside me, but I don't know what internal volume is being measured here.

He's a mirror, and I'm a bird who's mistaken him for a window. It's not the mirror's fault, and the bird can't help herself. In Charlie I see myself, and I see a way out. If I could only recognize my own reflection for what it is, all of this would stop.

For his birthday, I buy us tickets to see the same band that we saw the summer that we spent together in Seattle. It's been three years since I've seen this band, and I've turned thirty since then, and the opening band is so much younger looking than I can ever recall, and my head is spinning because of how quickly I have fallen through my twenties — as if I've been pushed through the open window of a high-rise only to bounce off the pavement, stunned and disoriented, but ultimately relatively unscathed.

The day after the concert, I sell three pairs of shoes to a secondhand store on State Street and use most of the ten dollars to see a matinee, a Woody Allen movie. It's the first time that I've ever seen a movie alone.

March 2011
San Diego, California

I'm here to fail some more tests and hopefully to use the data of those failures to make a new plan for strengthening my brain. Charlie is here with me, at this appointment with a specialist in unusual neurological cases, in part because I'm trying to prove something. I want him to see the doctors fussing over me in the hope that he will be forced to "get it" but mainly because I'm scared. When I feel overwhelmed by the spatial world, Charlie tries to comfort me by saying, "It's OK, you're just anxious." I don't know how to get him to understand my anxiety as a symptom instead of a cause. He didn't want to take the weekend away from schoolwork, and he especially didn't want to drive to San Diego, but he came anyway. Now that he's here with me in front of the specialist and a few of that specialist's grad students gathered around a long wooden table, I'm worried that I've made a mistake. I'm nervous about what they think of us; I'm worried that they're looking down on me for bringing someone with me. I can't even believe that this specialist has agreed to see me, and I'm afraid of not being the good patient.

The specialist's eyes are rimmed red, and he's thinner than he looked on the clips of his lectures and talk show interviews I found online. "What's most interesting," he says, "is actually how normal you are. You have extraordinarily few impairments for someone with such a large lesion. Anyone else, a stroke victim, with this, and the damage would have been severe." I'm reminded of an interview that I read with a woman who wrote a book about odd objects that people swallow, either intentionally or as part of a carnival act or accidentally. *I think it's partly the nature of that which is incongruous* was how she explained to the interviewer her fascination with people who swallow tacks, padlocks, swords, spoons. *Something appears where it's not supposed to appear. And there's this sense of "How did this possibly happen? It seems impossible."*

This is the first time that anyone has

wanted to study me for how normal I am. I feel somewhat ashamed for focusing on my incongruence rather than on how lucky I am to be so high functioning. I'm also uncomfortable with equating "normal" with "lucky."

The specialist says, "So am I to understand there is no urgent need here, that you are just curious?"

At first, I'm taken aback by the question. Is he accusing me of being a tourist? Worse, is he right? I have the same questions about consciousness — the unfathomably complex jive handshake between my brain and my mind — as anyone else does; I just have a better ice breaker.

"Well, I've had this my whole life, so I guess I can't say that it's urgent, but I am very, very confused in my daily life. If you could help me with that, I'd appreciate it."

"Then there's the issue of your depression or anxiety. You are worried about whether the atrophy will widen."

"Well, since no one knows how it began or ended, why couldn't it open up again?"

"It can't. Stop worrying."

I think of that old doctor joke: *Doctor, it hurts when I go like this. So stop going like that.*

The longer answer, I think, to what it

means to "stop going like that," is to become comfortable with not knowing. What I'm here trying to rewire is the most essential part of how I parse the world, my perception. It's hard to "stop going like that."

He starts pulling picture books of optical illusions from the bookshelf behind him, opening each one up and pointing to a specific jumble of shaded dots or maze of lines, each time asking, "Is there anything unusual about this to you?" About half of the time I see something, and half the time I don't. He and his graduate students are muttering "Interesting, interesting" to each other. "It's not Gerstmann's," he says. It never seemed to make much difference if I had Gerstmann's or not, since I know by now that there isn't a treatment specific to that diagnosis that's any different from the coping mechanisms that I've been trying. His phone rings, and he says, "I have to leave for a meeting. Do you have any more questions for me?"

"Do you think the anxiety actually has to do with this?"

I've managed to ask my question as obtusely as possible, but he understands what I want to know and is generous with me.

"No, that would be the temporal lobe.

Since you don't have any damage there, we have to assume that it is . . ." He trails off.

"Situational." I finish his sentence.

He nods and gets up to leave for his meeting.

We spend the next three hours just inside the UC San Diego campus entrance with an elfin graduate student. "OK," she says, "whenever a car comes, I want you to guess how many seconds until it will reach where you're standing; then we'll count together how many seconds until it actually reaches you."

Several cars later, we've learned that I am consistently several seconds late in my estimates. With this in mind, all I have to do is shave a few seconds off my original estimates in order to be correct. I think that the idea here is that as my guessing gets better, my experience of it will also become more accurate, so that eventually the guessing will recalibrate my internal estimations. We head out to a busy intersection to count more cars, where the vehicles veering toward me are so overwhelming that I find it difficult to focus on the task.

In her office in the basement of the university, she rips up pieces of tape to make a grid of the floor, then jots down a map on a folded sheet of paper for me to follow through the taped grid. "Don't move the map, only hold it straight in front of you as you follow it." After several attempts, the usual backtracking and retracing while holding the map stiffly in front of me, this task eventually proves impossible. I'm exhausted and weary, the way you would feel after cramming all night for a test. After the grid-on-the-floor test, the grad student says to me, "Oh, I think I get it! It's like you're in a foreign country all the time."

June 2011
Santa Barbara, California
The Invisible Disabilities Association Web
site doesn't offer much advice on whether
or not to disclose your disability in a job
interview other than "The decision to
disclose is yours. Do what feels comfortable."

I know Laura, the woman who's vacating
the position I'm applying for, because she's
dating someone in Charlie's program. "I
know that they're looking for someone
compulsively detail oriented," she tells me.

I nod quietly.

"I'm sure you'll get an interview," she goes
on, "because you're such a great fit."

A week later, I sit outside the Humanities
and Social Sciences Building at UCSB
rereading a book about how to prepare for
a job interview and swallow some herbal
antianxiety pills made from powderized

silkworms or mushroom caps; I forget which. I sit down, and the rest is a blur, but something must have gone right. It's a half-time position, but still, it's a start.

The day after I'm formally offered the job of programs and events coordinator for the Interdisciplinary Humanities Center at USCB by a man in Human Resources named Darwin ("If you get a call from Darwin, call him back ASAP. Darwin is in charge of selection," says Laura), Dr. Marsha Linehan appears on the front page of the *New York Times* Web site: "Expert on Mental Illness Reveals Her Own Fight." The founder of Dialectical Behavior Therapy, now sixty-eight, was once a seventeen-year-old in a locked ward. In the program, we used to mimic her stern drawl as she introduced a new behavior skill on the DVDs we had to watch each week in group. Who was this doctor with the paisley neck scarves, beamed into this cold spare treatment room to save us all? I had watched a clip of her giving a lecture, in which she said that she worked with suicidal patients because she needed the worst cases in order to prove that her program really worked. I thought I heard her snicker.

Even the group leader used to sing "Marsha, Marsha, Marsha" in that singsongy Brady Bunch imitation. Seeing a photo of Dr. Linehan's arms covered with cigar-sized burns and diagonal slashes feels like finding out that the girl you used to make fun of in the cafeteria goes home at night and rips her hair out.

We like to hear that our professional figures are vulnerable: the neurologist with Asperger's, the therapist with borderline personality disorder. It humanizes them. Does Marsha Linehan have imposter syndrome? Between patients did she ever sit slack-jawed at her new desk as I do, wondering how the hell she got herself into this? How is it that her references glowed about her, that her interview was like a slow-motion dream where she was soaring over the Grand Canyon? Did Marsha Linehan ever feel confused about how best to interpret "business casual"?

The balance of power that we need to believe in when sitting in a cold room in that thin hospital gown, legs dangling over the examining table, who or what we need to put our faith in to believe that we can be healed (that by merit of having bodies, we deserve to be healed), is slippery by function. Humans depend on other humans to heal and be healed. You wouldn't take your car to a mechanic who's never been in a crash, and I'd never take my heart to a therapist who hasn't broken one and had hers broken. In DBT, I always felt as if something integral was missing when Marsha was hologrammed in from DVDs. In the interview, she mentions the answer that she used to give patients who asked about the burns and cuts on her arms. "Do you want to know that I've suffered?"

When I type *imposter syndrome* into a search engine, the automated suggestions include:

Imposter syndrome graduate school
Imposter system academia
Imposter system test
Imposter system book
Imposter system cure

"How did you end up here?" my new boss asks. When I tell her that I followed Charlie, she says cheerfully, "I'm a trailer, too. My husband was at Yale when we got this call. People tend to stay here for a while; it's an easy place to be."

The blue of the ocean here is so rich that it's overwhelming, like International Klein Blue. The waves look stiff and thickly peaked, like a prop cardboard cake frosted for a TV commercial. It's the kind of

disarming beauty that makes one mistrustful; especially when viewed from the back
of a bus on my commute to work. Mainly, I
am suspicious of my own luck. I'm working
at a university that never would have accepted me as a student during an economic
period when most of the friends whom I
went to grad school with have gone straight
back to working retail if they are lucky. I
have business cards, a name plate in front
of my office door. My last name card previous to this position was threaded through a
shoelace and worn around my neck. The
job will act as a trellis, a supportive structure
to wind my concept of time around. It's also
an obligation that forces me to get dressed,
leave the house, and interact with people.

After I am at the Interdisciplinary
Humanities Center for a couple of weeks, I
am asked to run some papers to another
part of campus. "How is your sense of direction?" my boss asks.

"I . . . don't really have one," I say.

"That sort of thing is always interesting to
me, how people think differently . . ."

Laura must have mentioned something. I
tell her the whole story. In telling her about
my brain, I use my hands, first clasped
together and then slowly spread apart to
explain how the matter was pushed back by

291

the pooling reservoir of cranial fluid.

As part of my job responsibilities, I make a monthly calendar of events and update the Web site; I schedule a lecture series. I set up receptions and take them down. I make hotel reservations and order sandwiches and pour wine and raise my hand at the end of lectures to ask questions. At first, I think, *Oh god, what have I gotten myself into?* I set deadlines in the past instead of the future, or accidentally extend them by a month. It's exhausting, and for the first couple of months, every day I'm afraid that it will be my last.

"Babe, you've got to calm down," Charlie tells me. "You don't understand; this isn't some barista job. They can't just walk in and fire you. You could develop a crack addiction, go to rehab, and come back, and they still couldn't fire you. Relax."

This is especially generous of him because we're completely falling apart, although we're only beginning to admit it to ourselves. He is beginning to admit it to himself. I refuse to talk about it with anyone because I'm still convinced that I can fix it. I am the problem, my reactionary attitude, my insecurities and fears. This is good news, I think, because I can apologize, I can promise to get better, I can buy myself time, try harder, become an updated version of myself. If he cheated, as he often tells me he's considering, then he would be the problem. But he doesn't. He confesses his desires, feels better, and when his desires return — for a woman at the bar, a fellow grad student, a mutual friend — he confesses again. If only I was someone else, then he would want me. I have to become a stranger to him if I want to be known again.

At work, I stay late and come in early; I make drafts and revisions, I take breaks from deadline projects when I get too tired to see them correctly, and eventually I start to feel less like the Trojan horse sent to inadvertently take down the tiny civilization of the UCSB Humanities Center.

This is the first job where I am transparent about my disability and where I feel supported enough to ask for accommodations. My boss knows that if she orders a pizza for the lunch meeting and asks me to pick it up, I will need the total of the order from her beforehand in order to precalculate the proper tip on my phone. I think this is a kernel of what it means to be an adult; understanding your limitations and discerning from experience when to push yourself and when not to.

Rilke says "learn to love the questions." I

love my litter of neurological questions fiercely, and like most things we love, I sometimes resent them because I have no choice other than to love them. There's so little we know about the brain and even less about the mind. I tend to want to lean on the support of hard scientific facts about my brain, but in the end what I understand of my condition feels less medical and more like an alchemical blurring of philosophy and anatomy.

March 2012
Santa Barbara, California

In *The Odyssey,* the sea god Proteus punishes the king of Sparta for offending the gods by calming the winds that would carry the king's ship home. Proteus's daughter tells the king that if he can capture her father and hold on to him long enough, he will eventually tire and tell the king how to please the gods again, returning the wind to his sails. The king captures Proteus and holds on to him no matter what he changes into — a lion, a leopard, a pig, a serpent — until he finally becomes exhausted and relents. This is the name that Charles Proteus Steinmetz, the scientist with the twisted skeleton, chose for himself.

If I hold on tighter to the story that we are meant to be together, I am sure that it will become the truth. Charlie is shape-shifting as I clutch him, but my clasp only makes him thrash harder. Inevitably, I lose my grip.

Our therapist suggests that we should avoid all contact with each other for three months to a year; it takes us several failed attempts to actually stick to this. It feels like a performance piece. At CalArts, I read about the performance artist Marina Abramovic and her lover, Ulay, who ended their relationship by starting out on opposite ends of the Great Wall of China and walking toward each other to meet in the center. Once they met in the center of the Great Wall, they each said good-bye to the other and finished their walks.

We decide that I should be the one to leave. In April, I move to a room in a creaky Victorian less than a mile away from our old place. Upstairs from me is home to a former used bookseller, a violin maker, a bartender, a grad student, an aged yellow cat named Leelo, and thirty thousand books neatly shelved in the attic. The collection of books is also housed in the common space and the garage. My room is downstairs, next to a room that is used as office space for a real estate business run by the landlords (a father approaching his nineties and his sixtysomething son). I'm assured by the former bookseller that the landlords are almost never there, and that he will be picking up our rent checks. Anyone not blinded by that particular blend of urgency and grief known to the newly former live-in significant other can see where this arrangement is headed.

The real estate agent landlords are there constantly and it turns out the guy who picks up our rent is charging each roommate differing amounts in accordance with his mood. The real estate agents treat the house more as their vacation retreat than an office space; the Victorian has been in their family for generations, and they feel perfectly at home enjoying their morning coffee in the kitchen and opening the double doors to their office to include the parlor common space. My main objection is that to get to the bathroom in the morning, I have the option of either dodging the geriatric landlords enjoying their morning paper and coffee in the kitchen or attempting to exchange morning pleasantries with them while in my bathrobe. When I gently confront the former bookseller about this awkward situation, he says that there's nothing he can do about it. I'm out after a month and a half; most of my stuff is still at Charlie's since I haven't worked out a method to transport it all.

This time, my parents are driving down to help me. Charlie and I are only a couple of months into our latest attempt to avoid each other completely when we agree to meet at a posh bakery by his place to discuss logistics. It quickly spirals into a blowout fight, our biggest public argument ever, over whether my father can enter his house.

"I'm not comfortable with your father being in my house. This makes me really uncomfortable, the idea of him being in my house. I don't want him seeing my things. What if he touches my things?"

I don't know where the hell this is coming from. It's not news to me that he's particular about his possessions, but I never had any idea that Charlie was so intimidated by my dad. I forget that he has this effect on people outside of our family.

"If you're not going to help me move and you're not going to let him help me, how the hell am I supposed to get my stuff?"

I plead my case to our mutual therapist, who talks him down until he relents. It's May; the UCSB students are preparing to leave for the summer. The apartment units by campus are lined with sagging couches. I pick up secondhand Ikea furniture from outside sorority houses; my dad helps me load a used particleboard wardrobe into the back of the family minivan.

This time I move into a small studio with a loft bed, in a craftsman-style house that was originally cut into apartments to create housing for the nuns in the service of the church down the street. This seems like a woefully fitting landing for me to begin my newly single life in a small town with very few people my age. I use Charlie and my boss as references on my application. When the landlady finds out that I am on disability for a neurological condition, she calls Charlie for reassurance about my ability to get up and down from the loft bed. My parents, who were originally planning to drive down from Portland for a week to help me load everything out of Charlie's and into my new place, decide to stay for six weeks and sublet an apartment downtown. First, I load their minivan with the few boxes I had at the Victorian. "The feral cats here are actually very sweet," my dad tells me, stooping down to pet Leelo, who is rubbing at his legs. "You know, it's fine. Santa Barbara is fine. It's plastic, but everyone needs plastic." The first night alone in my new apartment, I discover that the previous occupant had stuck little glow-in-the-dark star stickers on the ceiling of the loft bed. It's my own tiny galaxy.

■ ■ ■ ■

Aside from glimpsing him at a distance in his car, I don't see Charlie all year, even though my new place is one mile away from the cottage we shared. I stay on the humanities side of campus; he stays on the science side. Since I avoid the places where we used to go to together, I have no way of knowing if he is doing the same. It's 2012, the year when a few fringe believers are making noises about the apocalypse, as predicted by an ancient Mayan calendar. If the world came crashing down that year, I wouldn't have noticed.

During the beginning of our separation, I filled out a questionnaire that's supposed to help me get some distance from my emotions.

If your feelings were a color, what color would they be?
Purple.

If your feelings had a shape, what shape would they be?
Egg.
A purple egg. A real shiner.

On the bus to work, every so often a driver

will ask me for my Medicare card. I use a "mobility" card, a card for disabled riders that you can only purchase by flashing your Medicare card and twenty dollars to a local transit authority worker who sits in a little booth in the transit office downtown. It would take a lot of effort to get a fake card, but this isn't about that; this is about a little game where the driver feels big and I feel small. I can't really explain why, even after I show him my card, I feel embarrassed. This small accusation that I'm not really the way that I am just hits too close to home for me.

Going to the grocery store is still my biggest hurdle. I try to go at off-hours when the store is the least crowded, and I remind myself to take my time, that no one cares how long it takes me to find the peanut butter. One afternoon while I'm running errands after work, the woman in front of me in line at the drugstore turns around to smile hesitantly at me, as if she wants to ask a question. I take my headphones off. "Are you from around here?" she asks. I smile and shake my head, the same answer that I give wherever I am.

She steps out of line to ask a clerk, I see the hand waving, hear her ask, "On the other side of the highway? Left? Are you sure?"

This will be my first full year of living independently without assistance from my parents, a boyfriend, or friends.

May 2013
Portland, Oregon

I'm back in town for a wedding. I make an appointment with Dr. Z, whom I haven't seen since I graduated from CalArts. His practice has grown to include another neurological chiropractor, a physical therapist, and an intern. The intern looks the same age that I was when I first saw Dr. Z, in his midtwenties. He sits in the back of the exam room and watches as Dr. Z runs me through some exercises.

"OK, walk down the hall and say the alphabet backward."

Trying to do both at once, I accompany each letter with a stiff galloping step, and I get tripped up by the letter *G*.

"OK, OK, back up. OK. This goes in your left hand now."

He places a small hand massager, green polka-dotted and shaped like a toy frog, in my hand and turns it on; it trembles.

"Now start over. Walk down the hall, alphabet backward."

I walk smoothly and recite the alphabet backward in its entirety.

"There you go. We just needed to juice up your brain a bit."

The intern cracks, "You're going to have to keep that frog in your hand forever now."

What does it mean for me to know that if you place a hand massager in my left hand I can walk down a hall and recite the alphabet backward at the same time, whereas I could not before? It means that there's still more to my brain than I understand, that I've witnessed undeniable change.

"We're going to have to get you down here more often," he says. "You just have such a damn cool brain."

In July, I'm back in my apartment in Santa Barbara when I break down crying after reading that Alan Turing, the engineer who Charlie told me killed himself by eating a chemical-laced apple, was posthumously pardoned by the UK parliament for the crime of homosexual activity. The feeling of being so deeply connected (to the passage of time, to Charlie, to powerful gestures that

come too little too late) and so alone
overwhelms me.

September 2013
Santa Barbara, California

A year and five months after we broke up, Charlie and I agree to meet over coffee in a park with a lake full of ducks and turtles, like the lake by his old apartment in Seattle. He tells me, "I know that I have a certain special insight into what's difficult for you," and I wince. I tell him that even if he's right, I would like some space now to also be a person whom he just met; that I'll try to do the same for him. I also want to tell him that I haven't forgotten the tone in his voice that means that he's in pain and doesn't want to talk about it. We were never very good at figuring out the difference between having an insight and applying one.

In November, I start going back to the bar that I avoided for a year for fear of running into Charlie. I meet a graduate student in history who collects orchids. I bluff my way through a conversation about different varieties; the Latin names feel both ancient and familiar coming out of my mouth, like a prayer or a spell. *Phalaenopsis, Cymbidium, Dendrobium.* I give him my card and tell him that he should get in touch with me if he wants his students to receive extra credit for attending the lecture series at the humanities center.

The time that I begin to spend with the grad student contains some kind of nutrient that I didn't know I'd been starving for; still, I can't stand to put my lot in with his. We've both broken up long-term relationships around the same time, and both feel ambivalent about starting anything new; now that I've lived on my own in Santa Barbara for the past year, this common anxiety feels heightened for me. The list of people who weren't sure that I'd be able to live independently includes my parents, Charlie, my therapist, my neurologist. My freedom is hard won and always at risk of receding; anything that threatens my solitude feels as if it also threatens my independence. The more whole I begin to feel on my own, the more mistrustful I've become of any of the traditional promises about what makes someone feel complete, especially in relationships. Learning to value my independence was a painful lesson, one that I'm scared of forgetting and even more frightened of having to learn all over again.

On one night he spends at my place he wakes me at 3:00 a.m., screaming "OhGodPleaseNoHelpMePleaseNoGod!" at the top of his lungs. My gut instinct is to put my hand against his chest to feel for blood. I can make out that his hands are in the air, but it's too dark for me to tell if he's guarding his face or about to throw a punch. I cautiously place my hand on his chest and find no blood anywhere, so I grab his arms by the wrists and shake him. "Are you all right? Are you all right?" I yell over and over. I'm so scared that I've forgotten his name. I finally shake him awake, and he turns his back to me and says quietly to the wall, "No."

I don't know if I should comfort him or leave him be. I honestly don't know if it's any of my business at all except that he happens to be in my bed. After watching someone whom I'm just starting to know and care for in so much pain, I feel terrified and helpless. I think that this must be how Charlie felt watching me, and I feel sick. At the time, I couldn't help any of it any more than if I had been asleep.

I know the shame and embarrassment of

your wildest self witnessed by someone you care for, and after being woken up by someone else's nightmare, I understand more deeply how it feels to be on the other end of things — when your care can't dampen someone else's pain.

After spending a year living alone, I have finally learned how to read my own vulnerabilities and address them. The space has allowed me very slowly to find gentleness toward the intensity of my own feelings instead of trying to violently expel them from my body. During this year, I have untangled my desires and resentments from Charlie's, slowly extricating what he actually felt from what I wished he felt. In my time alone, I've read books and listened to music made by artists who also feel deeply, and they have made me feel less alone and helped me find the courage to risk really knowing someone again.

In the morning, I don't ask him what the dream was about. I'm not ready to know, and some dark and ugly-feeling part of me resents him for breaking our contract — for not being someone "easy to be with" as he had offered to be months earlier, an agreement that given enough time I wouldn't have been able to keep either. I wonder if anyone could, and for how long.

Instead, I tell him that I used to have a recurring dream about the apocalypse. In the dream I know that it is the apocalypse because fire is creeping up streets from the burning buildings on the horizon. The only way to escape my dream apocalypse is to drive out of the dream city, so I get into the driver's seat of a car and strap on the seat belt. The dream ends the same way, every time. I crash my car and die before I get a block down the street.

When she was little, my friend Solen used to have a terrifying recurring nightmare in which her only escape from torture was to conjure a tall building to jump off of. Now she's an architect.

Everyone has a labyrinthine brain with a Minotaur at the center: a memory, an illness, a heartache, a deep frustration. Shake hooves with your Minotaur; invite your Minotaur to coffee. Your Minotaur is lonely and hungry and thus, understandably, not in the best of moods. No one understands what it's like to be a Minotaur; this is why he is writing a memoir. He says *testimony,* he says *witness,* and he speaks of his responsibility to the Minotaur community. You are not sure that the world really needs another memoir by a mythological being, one more man-beast identity crisis to stack on the pile, but you try to be supportive because he is the only Minotaur you have. You've heard of and seen people who claim to have slain their Minotaurs with trips to rehab or years of therapy, and while you admire them, it's also still a little sad. Maybe because when people are defined so long by struggle and battle, it's tough to know who they are once they've won. Once you get to the center of a labyrinth, you still have to find your way back out. You can't see anyone from where you're standing, but still you hope that there's someone listening through the other paper cup at the end of your twine, waiting by the exit sign. You hope that someone wants to know what's been taking so long. "Why the holdup?" You hope at least that someone noticed that you were gone.

The kicker here is that the person at the other end of the labyrinth, the person who you hope is waiting for you, cannot help you through. That person cannot guide you, tell you "No, your *other* left." All that the person at the end has signed up for is to wait for you; all that you can promise is to move forward. Waiting is enough; moving forward is enough.

Isn't what we all want, and what we're all

terrified of, is for someone to see us for our truest selves? As someone who relies on others, I have a physiological stake in empathy, and still I have to work hard to find it in myself for the same people whom I rely on. It's so hard to remember that while my perception is unique, my pain is not. In therapy, in relationships, in my writing, I've been looking for a map out of the pain of being human, but the word *atlas* means "to endure." No one is born with a map of life in hand. Just when we think that we know where we're headed, that's when the real trouble starts; the unforeseen circumstances, the self-sabotaging, the oasis on the horizon that melts into a mirage. The brain is often an unreliable narrator. It tells you go left, go right, trust this person, don't trust that one, you are weak, you are strong. You alone decide when to listen.

I have a friend whose therapist taught him to force himself out of his overwhelming thoughts and back into the present by talking to himself in his car, on the way to work. "This is me now. This is me talking. This is the sound of my voice." I'm already over-analyzing his strategy as he tells it to me. How can the sound of my voice anchor me in time? Once it leaves my body, pushed by my breath past the tongue, the teeth, I'm already trailing behind it.

I am the same as before I knew the truth about my brain, and I'll never be that person again; my diagnosis is both an ending and a beginning. I still type "Developmental Gerstmann's Syndrome" or "right parietal atrophy" into a search engine sometimes, to confirm my symptoms to myself — to be sure that I'm not making all of this up.

This is me now. This is the sound of my voice.

ACKNOWLEDGMENTS

My deepest gratitude to:

Fress Club: Mark, Lesley, Carly, and
Marni Cohen.

The Diamond Family: Ron, Linda, Jake,
and Danielle.

Henry Dunow and Wendy Owen, Caroline
Zancan and everyone at Henry Holt, Kristy
Rippee, Karl and Lenora Yerkes, Nora
Gedgaudas, Dr. Michael Mega, Dr. Glen
Zielinski, Dr. V. S. Ramachandran, Jon Wagner and the members of my CalArts thesis
class, David L. Ulin, Maggie Nelson,
Brighde Mullins, Leslie Brody, Joy Manesiotis, Bill McDonald, the Johnston Center
for Integrative Studies, UCSB's Interdisciplinary Humanities Center, and the
Corporation of Yaddo.

In memory of Connie Bowsher, the first teacher to have faith in me.

ABOUT THE AUTHOR

Cole Cohen holds an MFA in creative writing and critical studies from California Institute of the Arts. She was a finalist for the Bakeless Prize and the Association of Writers & Writing Programs prize in nonfiction. She currently lives in Santa Barbara, California, where she works at the University of California Santa Barbara's Interdisciplinary Humanities Center.

The employees of Thorndike Press hope you have enjoyed this Large Print book. All our Thorndike, Wheeler, and Kennebec Large Print titles are designed for easy reading, and all our books are made to last. Other Thorndike Press Large Print books are available at your library, through selected bookstores, or directly from us.

For information about titles, please call:
  (800) 223-1244

or visit our Web site at:
  http://gale.cengage.com/thorndike

To share your comments, please write:
  Publisher
  Thorndike Press
  10 Water St., Suite 310
  Waterville, ME 04901